Great Companies,
Great Charts

Great Companies, Great Charts

◆

Effective Stock Trading Techniques to Beat the Markets

Andy Dunn

iUniverse, Inc.

New York Lincoln Shanghai

Great Companies, Great Charts
Effective Stock Trading Techniques to Beat the Markets

iUniverse, Inc.

For information address:
iUniverse, Inc.
2021 Pine Lake Road, Suite 100
Lincoln, NE 68512
www.iuniverse.com

ISBN: 0-595-31275-6 (pbk)
ISBN: 0-595-66288-9 (cloth)

Printed in the United States of America

Statement of non-liability

Investing in the stock market is risky. The information in this book expresses only the opinions of the author…that's me. Take what I say with a bag of salt. No representation is made that any account will, or is likely to, achieve profits or losses similar to those shown. There are differences between theory and actual results achieved by any particular trading system. Theoretical trading does not involve financial risk, and therefore cannot account for the reality of actual trading. Past performance is not an indicator of future performance. The stocks I currently hold, have held in the past, and will buy in the future, do not represent a recommendation to buy, hold, or sell. The risk of loss in trading stocks can be substantial. If, while attempting to apply any of the ideas, procedures, or advice contained within this book, you suffer loss, you are wholly responsible. I disclaim responsibility for your actions, and for your loss.
What I'm saying is, if you bet the farm and lose, "you" bet the farm.

Andy Dunn

Chart Permissions

The stock price charts used throughout this book were created courtesy of StockCharts.com. They allow users to reprint up to 25 charts a day (some restrictions apply). StockCharts.com has simply the Web's best financial charts.
http://stockcharts.com.
The compounding interest growth chart in chapter 18 is used with written permission from Bob Sardis at MoneyChimp.com. Money Chimp offers some of the Web's best financial calculators. http://www.moneychimp.com.

To Mom and Dad

Contents

Acknowledgements

I owe many thanks to my friends and family whose support and ideas helped shape this book. My friends were instrumental in locating a chart source, correcting grammar and picking a book title. I can't wait to write the runner-up title, *DUNN ON STOCKS: Frisky Fireball Trading*. I also wish to thank my copyeditor, Denise. Special thanks to Paul Cheatham, accountant and friend, for sitting me down a long time ago, and telling me the tall tale, *The Power of Compounding Interest*.

PART I

Online Screening for Winning Stocks

Introduction

Like many investors, my stock portfolio was crushed in the years 2000, 2001, and 2002. I had chest pains and migraines as I helplessly watched my retirement portfolio—$900,000—evaporate as the market relentlessly trended lower. It was during those years I forced myself to reevaluate how I traded. I created the mechanical, trend-following system I use today. By using the techniques described in this book, my portfolio has almost fully recovered. Within the next couple years, it should reach new highs. This book details the successful strategies I now use to invest in the stock market.

Why This Book is Unique

The book is unique for three reasons:

It's a blend of both fundamental and technical stock analysis.
It's a blend of both stock and futures trading techniques.
It's not just about stock picking, but a complete trading philosophy,

Most books on trading choose either a fundamental approach, dealing with accounting and financial statements, or a technical approach, dealing with stock chart price patterns. There are benefits using a synthesis of the two methods.

I invest in both stocks and futures. There are many excellent futures trading techniques that apply well to the stock market. By combining skillful stock-picking techniques with future trading's entry and exit techniques, a powerful trading system can be created.

Wall Street writers often focus on "stock picking." Picking the winners is only one part successful trading. Investors need to manage the whole trade from start to finish. Investors need self-discipline and confidence to trade without emotional interference. The standardized routines I use create investor competence.

Background in Risk Reward

I completed an undergraduate Bachelor of Business Administration (BBA) at Sir Wilfrid Laurier in Canada and then continued with a Masters of Business Administration (MBA) at University of California at Riverside. My focus was advertising. Near the end of my studies, I began to concentrate on market research. Market research is rooted in statistics, which is where I fell in love with probability theory. Gambling, speculating, and investing are essentially risk vs. reward—the heart of probability theory. There is a reason why CDs pay 2% and solid indexed mutual funds pay 10% or more—the greater the risk, the greater the chance of loss, and the greater the reward.

After university, I opened a series of small businesses. Some did poorly, some broke even, and a couple did well. I invested $35,000 in a dial-up Internet bulletin board system and lost it all. I invested $70,000 in a bar game vending route and broke even. I invested $55,000 in an instant sign store and sold the business seven years later for $215,000. I invested $70,000 in an Internet-based banner advertising system and sold it two years later for $1,000,000. These business events demonstrated:

With calculated risk can come reward.
Often two investments will make as much as eight others combined.
Never stop trying.

I began investing in the stock market with mutual funds in the early '90s. I eventually began trading stocks. Like most investors, I did well during the technology bubble of the late '90s and, like most investors, I was trapped as the market crashed. I didn't give up. I honed my risk-reward skills and applied them to the markets, developing my simple and unique trading style. My portfolio has beaten the market ever since.

Trading Philosophy

The stock market is as much about human nature as it is about financial statements, and moves up and down for many reasons. The stock market is about people—investors like you and I. We are creatures of habit. The markets have trended upward for the last century at a 10% clip and I think this trend will continue. There will always be stocks that out perform the market; the key is finding the characteristics of these winning stocks.

A good trading system does not need to be complex. Complexity often comes dangerously close to curve-fitting; customizing trading rules to a degree that realistic results are unlikely. Simple trading systems work, and are usually more robust over time. Most people do poorly in the market, not because of poor stock picking skills, but because of a lack of self-discipline. A trend following, mechanical system is one of the best tools for encouraging a complete, self-discipline, approach to investing.

The title of this book is *Great Companies, Great Charts* and my premise for writing the book is to give readers new skills for achieving "great returns."

1

Panning for Gold

Technical and Fundamental Analysis

The tech boom was on! The year was 1999 and the public had an insatiable thirst for stocks known as the dot-coms. Entrepreneurial fortune had smiled on me the previous year when I sold a banner advertising Web site for one million dollars. I invested these proceeds in the stock market. I quickly purchased 10 stocks. Like many investors, the system I used for choosing stocks was based on wild rumors, hot tips, and the seat of my pants. I was tossing dice in the big casino; when you choose to gamble, the casino always wins.

I decided to buy shares in an interesting new company called NetBank, Inc., (NASDAQ: NTBK). I was an Internet proponent and it made perfect sense that the public would eventually bank online. It never occurred to me that brick-and-mortar banks would simply create Web sites! That year, the price of NetBank went up eight fold. I made more than $200,000 (on paper) in three weeks, and had daydreams of purchasing my first Tropical island. I held NetBank all the way up! I held tightly onto NetBank all the way down. Down. Down. Down.

This rise-and-fall story repeated itself with most technology stocks and almost all the dot-com stocks. All but a handful of dot-coms exist today. From 2000 through 2002, I watched the majority of my portfolio go up in smoke. It was during these painful down years that I continued to read every investment book I could get my hands on while back testing hundreds of technical trading systems. I eventually came to the point where my investing was no longer about hot tips and gambling, but instead focused on logic, risk tolerance, human nature, and self-discipline.

In the following pages, I'll describe my investment methods for you. I make my living trading stocks. Discretionary trading relies on one's judgment, where mechanical trading relies on definite rules. I trade mostly mechanically which encourages self-discipline. My market philosophy is sensible and simple. The techniques I use can be adjusted to match your personal risk tolerance.

In the midst of the difficult years following the tech boom, I developed a clean model which uses both fundamental and technical analysis to place publicly-traded companies into one of four categories: great companies with great charts, great companies with weak charts, weak companies with great charts, and weak companies with weak charts.

Fundamental analysis is a method of anticipating future stock price movement using economic data. This data includes earnings, profit margins, and revenue growth. Technical analysis is a method of anticipating future stock price movement using price activity or chart patterns.

In a perfect world, pure fundamentalists believe companies with large profit margins and strong earnings should be the best stocks to purchase. Fortunately, this is not a perfect world—it's the stock market. Great companies don't always have the best performing stocks.

In a perfect world, pure technicians believe all knowable information for any given stock is logically reflected in that stock's price movement. Simply find the charts with upward price patterns and buy. Fortunately, this is not a perfect world—it's the stock market. Great charts don't necessarily indicate the company represented by the chart is financially sound. If you only cared about upward price momentum, then the dot-com stocks of the late '90s would be very attractive.

The stock market is made up of people. People buy and sell stocks for many reasons; some of which are emotional and irrational. While riding down the elevator in the Waldorf Towers, Sally overhears Bob-the-Bellhop tell Desk-Clerk-David that BioBioBio Inc., is a month away from finding a cure for the common cold. Sally just bought 1000 shares of BioBioBio Inc., and is currently deciding how she'll decorate her yacht moored in the Cayman Islands. Sally buys stock like many investors: trusting hot tips, hunches, and intuition. This style of investing is dangerous at best. However, by understanding fundamental and technical analysis, Sally would choose better stocks by finding the great companies with great charts.

The financial strength of a company is weak or great based on a fundamental evaluation provided by online stock screening tools. Stock screening allows investors to quickly scan large volumes of stocks using a series of filters or rules. The stock price activity of a company is weak or great based on a technical evaluation of its price charts. The chart below is a visual representation of my market model.

	Low	High
High	Great Companies Weak Charts	Great Companies Great Charts
Low	Weak Companies Weak Charts	Weak Companies Great Charts

Profitability and Growth
Fundamental Analysis

Low   High

Stock Price Activity
Technical Analysis

There are traders successfully buying and selling stocks in all four categories. I believe one quadrant offers superior equity choices over the others. If you want to pick more winners, search for great companies with great charts. These stocks are the bee's knees and have both technical and fundamental indicators suggesting they are more likely to move upward.

In the past 10 years ago or more, stock market research was done almost entirely by hand. Reading through financial statements, hand drawing price charts, calculating ratios, and moving averages, was tedious and time consuming. Computers and the Internet now offer investors powerful research tools that can do the same research in a fraction of the time. One of the most exciting tools is the online stock screener. The results from these screens are the stocks that best match your trading philosophy criteria. The first section of this book (chapters one through eight), revolve around stock screening. If you would like a sneak peek at some of my favorite screening Web sites, please visit these links:

http://screen.morningstar.com/StockSelector.html
http://screen.yahoo.com/stocks.html
http://www.quicken.com/investments/stocks/search/full/
http://moneycentral.msn.com/investor/finder/customstocks.asp

The Four Categories

Weak companies with weak charts are garbage. These companies are technically weak and fundamentally weak. This is the worst possible category for finding winning stocks. This is the land of the penny stock. This is the land of the dying company. This is the land of hyped startup. There is nothing to be found here but long shots. These companies have nasty financial statements and ugly chart patterns. If you want to find these companies using an online stock screener, enter criteria along the lines of:

Previous Day's Closing Price <= $10
Previous Day's Closing Price <= 52 Week Low
Net Profit Margin <= 0

Weak companies with great charts are technically strong, but fundamentally weak. If you care only about stock price, these companies will attract you. The dot-coms are a perfect example of weak companies with great charts. People usually purchase these stocks with the future hope of profitability. I don't like to buy on hope. Like most investors, I got punched in the gut during the dot-com crash and learned a hard lesson of life. If you want to find these companies using an online stock screener, enter criteria like:

Net Profit Margin <= 5
Previous Day's Closing Price >= 52 Week High

Great companies with weak charts are technically weak, but fundamentally strong. These companies offer sound financial statements with a beat down stock price. The public is not always rational. Stocks can be in fashion one year and old news the next. Some industries are sexier than others. Assuming the fundamentals were equivalent, if you had the choice between Super Sonic Microchip Inc., or White Pulp and Paper Inc., which stock would you buy? The public likes sizzle with their steak. Not all great companies are popular. Currently, a great company with a weak chart is the Microsoft Corporation (NASDAQ: MSFT). Microsoft has stunning financial statements. Most CEOs would kill for a 30% net profit margin—yet the share price of Microsoft has struggled in recent years.

Warren Buffet, one of the greatest stock market investors of modern times, is the king of finding great companies selling at bargain prices. He is a master of finding fundamentally sound companies with technically weak share prices.

Dogs of the Dow is an investment strategy that searches for stocks in this quadrant. This strategy has several variations, each attempts to choose good industrial companies with beaten down stock prices.

I don't fish for great companies with weak charts, but many successful investors do. If you want to find these companies using an online stock screener, enter criteria like:

Net Profit Margin >= 10
% Price Change YTD (or 12 months) <=0
Previous Day's Closing Price >= 10

Great companies with great charts are technically strong *and* fundamentally strong. Profit margins are thick; earnings are strong and growing. The share prices for these companies are headed up and right. These are the stocks I like. These are the stocks I want to hold. In the coming chapters, I'll show you in detail how to find these companies using online stock screening tools.

The Stock Market is a Competition

The stock market is a competition with thousands of players competing daily. If you trade equities, then you and I are players in this stock market game. Imagine for a moment you've been given $50,000,000 to buy players to build the best basketball team. It doesn't have to be basketball. Pick your favorite sport…soccer, football, NASCAR, etc. What players will you select?

Do you want low-priced weak players? These players are definitely a bargain. You'll save a lot of coin for nice jerseys and maybe a team jet. There is only one problem—your team sucks! Cheap, weak players are going to end up last in the league.

Do you want high-priced weak players? These players are due! This is the year they are going to shine. I know they have been using a special exercise machine and have these new trick sneakers that will make them go fast and strong. Weak players with high prices are long shots. Vegas is for gambling.

Do you want low-priced great players? Low-priced great players are difficult to find. If they are truly great, their price will quickly be corrected. It might be hard to find a full team of these rare jewels. Often these are great players past their prime. They will always be better than the average player, but they'll never be what they once were.

Do you want high-priced great players? Yes. These are the players that are going to win. There is a reason top athletes are paid big salaries—because they're worth it.

Great companies with great stock charts offer the best opportunity for finding winners. If a stock goes from $20 to $200, it gets there one dollar at a time, setting new highs all the way up. It's never a bargain.

2

The Mother Lode

Net Profit Margins, EPS Growth, and Stock Charts

Find companies with strong fundamentals and strong technicals and you've found the Mother Lode. Fundamentally, I look at profit margins and earnings per share (EPS); technically, I look at stock price charts and EPS bar charts.

Net profit margin has always been my favorite fundamental indicator. Great companies have above average profits. Higher net profits should mean the management team is more efficient, the product lines are superior, and the company is doing a better job than their competition.

For example: Business No. 1 grosses $10M a year and brings $200,000 to the bottom line. Business No. 2 grosses $1M a year and brings $200,000 to the bottom line. Given only this information, which of the two businesses would you prefer to own?

Number. 1 has a net profit margin of 2% and No. 2 has a net profit margin of 20%. I want to own business No. 2 because No. 1 has problems. Business No. 1's industry might be mature and price competitive. The management team might be inefficient or living high on the hog. There may be too many employees. The product lines might be inferior. There is no room for error with a 2% margin. Business No. 2 has everything going for it. No. 2 may be in an emerging growth industry. No. 2 might have a semimonopoly. The management team is more likely tight and efficient. The product lines are probably stronger. There is room to weather the odd storm.

Earning per share is my second favorite fundamental indicator. Great companies are growing companies. I want to see revenues growing year over year, and I want to see earnings growing year over year. Growth is good. When you purchase a stock, you're often speculating on the future growth of that company. Publicly-traded companies use the money generated from the sale of stock to accelerate growth and expansion.

A stock price going from the lower left-hand corner to the upper right-hand corner of a chart, with as flat a pattern as possible is my favorite technical indicator. I prefer finding stocks making new highs with a steady pattern leading up to that high.

Three Real World Examples

Here are real world examples of great companies with great charts. These are the types of companies I want to find and own. Try these symbols at your favorite online charting site.

Forest Laboratories, Inc., (NYSE: FRX), develops, manufactures, and sells both branded and generic drug products for prescription and over-the-counter sales. The fundamentals for Forest Laboratories are excellent. Their net profit margin is currently 29.60%. The EPS growth rates ytd vs. ytd is 36.60%. Technical analysis of FRX is also strong. The three-month stock chart goes from the lower left corner to the upper right corner as does the three-year chart. This is a great company with a great stock chart.

Shuffle Master, Inc., (NASDAQ: SHFL), develops, manufactures, and sells automatic card shufflers for casinos. Shuffle Master has an excellent net profit margin of 25.10%. The EPS growth rates ytd vs. ytd is 12.20%. Both the three-month and three-year stock charts are headed up and right. This is a great company with a great stock chart.

Boston Properties, Inc., (NYSE: BXP), is a self-managed real estate investment trust (REIT). Boston Properties has a net profit margin of 35.80%. Their EPS growth rates year-to-date vs. year-to-date is 64.80%. Both the three-year and three-month stock charts are headed up and right. This is a great company with a great stock chart.

These are the companies I want to own. These companies are stock market gold.

Firing on all Cylinders

My approach to stock picking combines the fundamental business indicators with the technical stock price indicators. A stock with both factors pushing it upward is firing on all cylinders. It has the engine power to keep climbing.

I'm not comfortable buying a stock because of its great balance sheet. This completely ignores the fact that traders are emotional. More than just accounting influences the people who play the stock market game. The book by author

Charles Mackay, *Extraordinary Popular Delusions & the Madness of Crowds*, details the large-scale irrational madness of people during a craze. The Tulip Bulb mania of 1624 is really no different than the dot-com frenzy of the late 1990s. Investors are emotional and not always rational.

I'm uncomfortable buying a stock simply because the share price is headed up or is repeating a chart pattern.

> *"As a science, I should say that chart reading shares a pedestal with astrology; but most chart readers are educated men and have too much mental discipline to take astrology seriously."*
>
> —Fred Schwed Jr., *Where Are the Customers' Yachts?*

Investors searching for companies using both technical and fundamental criteria will have the best chance of picking winners. These stocks are financially strong and technically popular.

3

Simple Stock Screening Rules

Online Screening Tools

In the next two chapters, I'll show how I screen for stocks. This is the fundamental portion of company research. In chapter 5, I'll show how I take the stock screener results and weed them down further using basic chart reading. This is the technical side of company research. I try to find 50 to 100 stocks during first screen, depending on market conditions. In an up-trending market, I'll find more stocks, and in a down-trending market I'll find less. I reduce the list of 100 prospects to 10 by looking at the price charts and EPS graphs.

Many Web sites offer free stock screening tools. These tools vary from simple to complex. Even basic screeners can help you quickly produce a short list of stocks for consideration. Here are four, free stock screener Web sites. I've listed some of the search criteria available. These lists might seem long and complex, but don't have a conniption fit—in the end, we will only use three or four rules for the basic search, and five to seven rules for the pro-level search. Most screeners offer enough parameters to make you hurl. It's refreshing to know that our basic search will be relatively simple, yet robust.

The *Morningstar Stock Screener* at
http://screen.morningstar.com/StockSelector.html is a basic screener that is easy to use. You can set your own criteria or select a Morningstar screen. This screener offers the following criteria:

- Stock sector

- Morningstar stock type

- Morningstar equity style box

- Minimum market capitalization

- Growth grade

- Profitability grade

- Financial health grade

- 3-year revenue growth greater than or equal to

- Return on equity (ROE) greater than or equal to

- 5-year forecasted earnings growth greater than or equal to

- YTD total return

- 1-month total return

- 3-month total return

- 1-year total return

- 5-year total return

- Trailing P/E ratio less than or equal to

- P/E-to-Earnings Growth Ratio (PEG) less than or equal to

- Dividend yield greater than or equal to

The *Yahoo! Finance Stock Screener* at http://screen.yahoo.com/stocks.html is another easy to use yet slightly more advanced screener that offers various selection criteria:

- Industry

- Index Membership

- Share Price

- Avg. Share Volume

- Market Cap

- Dividend Yield

- 1 Yr. Stock Perf

- Beta (Volatility)

- Sales Revenue

- Profit Margin

- Price/Earnings Ratio

- Price/Book Ratio

- Price/Sales Ratio

- PEG Ratio

- Est. 1 Yr. EPS Growth

- Est. 5 Yr. EPS Growth

- Avg. Analyst Rec.

- Display info for

The *Quicken.com Stock Search Full Search* screener at http://www.quicken.com/investments/stocks/search/full/ is more powerful and offers many selection criteria:

- Industry Class(es)

- S&P Index Membership

- EPS

- Market Cap

- P/E Ratio

- PEG Ratio

- Price to Book

- Price to Sales

- Dividend Yield

- 1 yr. EPS Growth

- 3 yr. EPS Growth

- 5 yr. EPS Growth

- 1 yr. Revenue Growth

- 3 yr. Revenue Growth

- 5 yr. Revenue Growth

- 1 yr. Income Growth

- 3 yr. Income Growth

- 5 yr. Income Growth

- Consensus Ratings

- Latest Qtr Earnings Surprise

- Earnings Growth Avg. Est. Next 5 Yrs.

- Forward P/E

- Revenue/Employee

- Income/Employee

- Current Ratio

- Quick Ratio

- Net Profit Margin

- LTD/Equity Ratio

- LTD/Assets Ratio

- Revenue

- Market Share

- Total Return, 5 yr.

- Return on Assets

- Return on Equity

- Price

- Beta

- Relative Strength

- % Held by Institutions

- % Held by Insiders

My favorite free stock screener is the *MSN Money Custom Stock Search* located at http://moneycentral.msn.com/investor/finder/customstocks.asp and it is the cat's meow. There are more than 100 criteria available to design custom stock searches. This screener is flexible and powerful. The only complaint I've heard about this screening tool is its steep learning curve. It can be intimidating at first. Playing with the predefined searches can quickly help you learn how to set up the rules. Predefined power searches are available at moneycentral.msn.com/investor/finder/predefstocks.aspx. The power searches are divided into Technical Screens and Fundamental Screens.

Professional level subscription based stock screeners are available online. One that garners many positive reviews is ProSearch by *Wall Street City Pro* located at http://www.wallstreetcity.com/tools/tools_main.html and offers more than 300 search criteria with the ability to back test results. Back testing reveals how your strategy fared in the past. ProSearch is currently $9.95 a month. *Investors Business Daily* at http://www.investors.com also offers a professional level Custom Screen Wizard. This tool is available for $45.75 a month.

Three Rules for a Simple Screen—The 20/20/20

Traders often believe that a stock or futures trading system or screening method needs to be complex. Adding more rules and complexities often begins to curve-fit the data. Curve-fit systems customize the trading rules to a degree that they produce unrealistic and improbable results. Good screens are simple, logical, profitable, and not overly optimized. This produces robust results.

1. Stock price is greater than or equal to $20

2. Net profit margin is greater than or equal to 20%

3. EPS growth year vs. year is greater than or equal to 20%

The first rule is based on a minimum stock price. This rule is designed to avoid the dangers of low-priced equities. There is a den of thieves lurking in the stock market. These thieves can be found trading penny stocks. Buy stocks above $20 and save yourself from a world of hurt. Most investors consider any stock under $5 a penny stock. William J. O'Neil, author of *How to Make Money in Stocks* writes, "I do not like to buy any common stock that sells below $10 to $12 a share. If you want to fly, why not go first class?"

I prefer a larger margin of safety and consider stocks under $20 to be penny stocks. This may seem extreme, but if I said $12, some might be tempted to buy $9. If I said $15, some might be tempted to buy $10. If I said $20 then most will stay above $15. I personally do not buy any stocks under $20. If a great company has a stock that is going to go from $10 to $200, I don't mind missing the little jaunt from $10 to $19. I'll catch the stock at $20 and ride it from there.

The second rule is based on a minimum net profit margin. Great companies bring more money to the bottom-line. The net profit margin is an important indicator of business strength and health. Find the companies with above average net profit margins and you'll find companies beating their competition. Net profit margins of 5% do not set my pants on fire. Net profit margins of 10% are nice, but I want better than nice. Net profit margins of 15% are great. Net profit margins of 20% make me pee my frilly white panties. These are the exceptional companies I want to find.

The third rule is based on growth. Great companies grow. Not only do they grow revenues, but they also grow earnings. Growing earnings provide the foundation for future stock price growth. I want to find companies with earnings per share up at least 20% year over year.

Let's try the Simple Screen!

Each online screening tool is slightly different. Here is how I would use the simple 20/20/20 on three of the online screeners listed earlier. I like the screens to deliver 50 to 150 prospective stocks at this stage. Each screener phrases the criteria in slightly different ways.

The *Quicken.com Stock Search Full Search* produced 152 results using:

- 1 yr. EPS Growth: Min 20%
- Net Profit Margin: Min 20%
- Price Min $20

The *Yahoo! Finance Stock Screener* produced 126 results using:

- Share Price $20 Min

- Profit Margin 20% Min

- Est. 1 Yr. EPS Growth: up more than 20%

The *MSN Money Custom Stock Screener* produced 144 results using:

- Net Profit Margin >=20

- Previous Days Closing Price >=20

- EPS Growth Year vs. Year >= 20

Using the screened results, I'll next go through the list, looking at each stock's three-month and three-year price charts. I'll also look at the EPS bar graphs if available. (I'll provide full details and diagrams on these techniques in chapter 5.)

4

Pro-Level Stock Screening Rules

The Fundamental Rules

In this chapter two more rules are added to the earlier simple search criteria. I soften the minimum requirements as more rules are added. These five rules help find financially successful companies. Ones where revenue growth is strong, earnings growth are strong, return on equity is strong, and net profit margins are strong.

1. Previous day's closing price is greater than or equal to $20

2. Net profit margin is greater than or equal to 15%

3. EPS growth year vs. year is greater than or equal to 15%

4. Revenue growth year vs. year is greater than or equal to 15%

5. Return on equity is greater than or equal to 15%

The Technical Rules

Previous day's closing price is near 52 week high

This optional rule is not as important as the five above and is not available from all screeners. This rule can be added to save time by reducing the list of prospective stocks to only the ones nearing their 52 week highs. I only buy stocks when they're making new highs. The reasons for this will be explained later.

Let's Try the Pro-Level Screen!

This time I will use the MSN Money Screener and Quicken.com screeners. The other free screeners don't offer some of the necessary parameters.

The *Quicken.com Stock Search Full Search* produced 85 results using:

- 1 yr. EPS Growth 15%
- 1 yr. Revenue Growth 15%
- Net Profit Margin 15%
- Return On Equity 15%
- Price Min $20

The *MSN Money Custom Stock Screener* produced 70 results using:

- Previous Day's Closing Price is greater than or equal to $20
- Return On Equity is greater than or equal to 15%
- Net Profit Margin is greater than or equal to 15%
- EPS Growth Year vs. Year is greater than or equal to 15%
- Rev Growth Year vs. Year is greater than or equal to 15%

By using two more rules with slightly softer parameters, I've effectively cut the list in half. This is a short list of great companies I now search through to find the few with great charts.

5

Pro-Level Screening Part 2

Three-Year and Three-Month Stock Charts

The screening techniques from the earlier chapters produced a list of stock candidates. I now take that list and go through each stock, looking at the three-year and three-month stock price history.

The three-year history provides a medium term look at the price activity. I want to find companies with stock prices that have performed well historically. It's difficult for companies to maintain strong profit margins and above average growth forever. Looking back more than three years makes it difficult to find big winners as economic forces begin to erode competitive advantages. Views greater than three years can also place the company in a previous business cycle with market conditions that don't exist today. One-year charts don't provide enough historic data. Three years is just right: Not too long and not too short for a larger view of stock price activity.

In the short term, I prefer looking at three months of data. This is a larger view than many traders are accustomed. This is not day trading, this is investing. Hours, days, and weeks are simply too short. When I want excitement, I go to Vegas. When I want to do well in the stock market, I look at the three-month and three-year stock charts.

For any stock chart, make sure the display scale is set to logarithmic. Log graphs show percentage changes, where arithmetic graphs do not. It's percentage change that's important. More and more investing Web sites are setting their default scales to logarithmic.

There are two main criteria I want to see when looking at the three-year and three-month stock charts. These are:

1. The graph moves from the lower left corner toward the upper right; and

2. The graph is as smooth as possible.

When a graph moves from the lower left corner to the upper right corner, this represents a stock growing in price over time. Such a company is having an excellent stock run. These companies should continue to climb in the future.

The smoother the graph the more stable the stock. I don't mind sleeping with one eye open, but I don't want to sleep with two eyes open. A flat price pattern is a good thing. Sometimes traders will say, "You can lay a ruler on that chart." Stable, historic growth is a good predictor of stable future growth. Random and historically wild growth shows instability. Here is an example of a good three-year stock chart.

Chart courtesy of StockCharts.com

Here is an example of a good three-month stock chart.

Chart courtesy of StockCharts.com

The three-month charts generally appear jagged and less stable than the three-year charts. I allow the three-month charts more freedom when analyzing them. This chart for Hot Topic Inc., (NASDAQ: HOTT) has greater volatility, but is still good.

Chart courtesy of StockCharts.com

Revenue and EPS Charts

After examining the three-year and three-month price charts, I finish my research with a review of each company's revenue and earnings per share data. Few financial sites offer revenue and EPS graphs for publicly-traded companies. I like the ones available at *MSN Money*. These are bright, bold bar graphs. A picture is worth a thousand words. The companies I'm searching for have:

Steady revenue and EPS growth for three years.

   When looking at quarterly EPS and revenue bar charts, I like finding patterns that resemble a set of stairs which lead up and right. This demonstrates smooth and stable quarterly growth, year over year. Keep in mind, not all companies have billing cycles that create stair step patterns. The key is finding companies that, year over year, continually grow when comparing quarters.

   I want to find companies with steady and stable growth, as well as a minimum percentage growth. If you can't locate quarterly EPS charts online, you can use EPS percentage increase rules for one year, two years, and three years. The graphs visually tell the story with greater meaning.

The Good, the Bad, and the Ugly

Here are examples of good, bad, and ugly charts. The line graphs below represent three-month and three-year price charts, the bar graphs represent three years of quarterly EPS.

   For price activity, the Good charts start at the lower left corner and end in the upper right corner. Zigzags are okay in moderation. The angle of the line might seem important since that can indicate stronger growth, but for now, we will focus on general trends. Two or more stocks can always be compared later using an investment growth chart to determine the better performer. The concern at this stage is to find charts starting at the lower left corner and going to the upper right corner and exhibit as much stability as possibly. Here are six good charts. The X-axis is time, the Y-axis is price. Below are Good chart patterns.

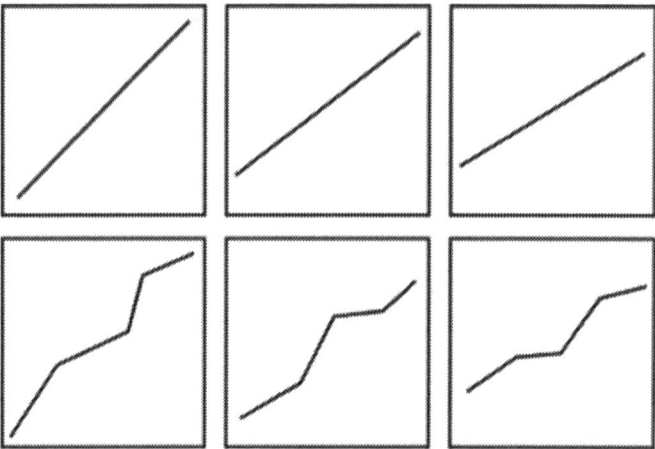

The Bad charts start in the upper right corner, but zig and zag all over tarnation. They might start in the upper left corner, zoom downward, and finish in the upper right. This would be a "U" shaped graph. "M", "W", and "U" shaped graphs are bad graphs—avoid them. Here are six bad charts. The X-axis is time, the Y-axis is price. Below are Bad chart patterns.

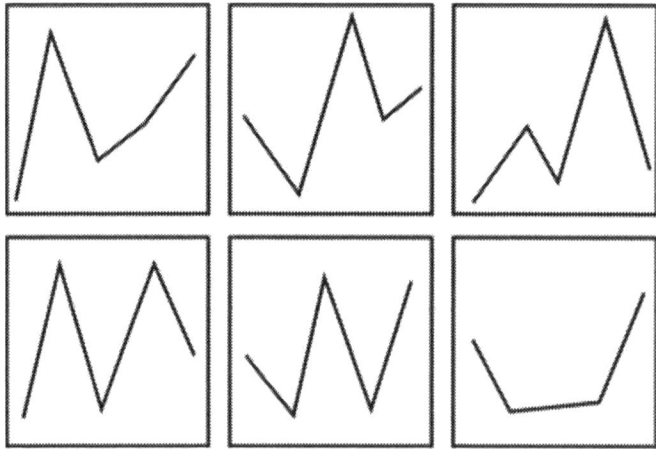

The Ugly charts below start in the upper left corner and end in the lower right corner. These charts have toilet paper written all over them. These patterns make shorter sellers giddy as grade nine girls. If I was shorting the market, these are the ugly charts I'd want to find Avoid these patterns. Here are six ugly charts. The X-axis is time, the Y-axis is price. Below are Ugly chart patterns.

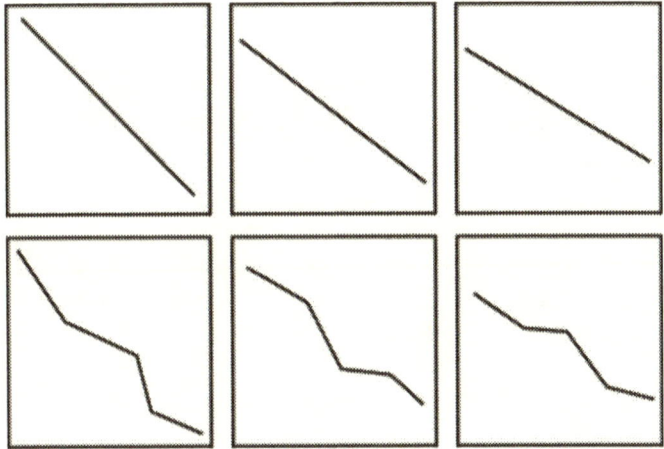

Remember I place tighter demands on the three-year graphs. These charts need to be the most stable. The three-month charts don't have to be as tight, and can be judged with more leniency.

Next are examples of good revenue and EPS bar graphs. The chart below is the classic stair step pattern. Each bar represents one quarter, and the four bars together represent a fiscal year. The X-axis is time and the Y-axis is revenue or earnings.

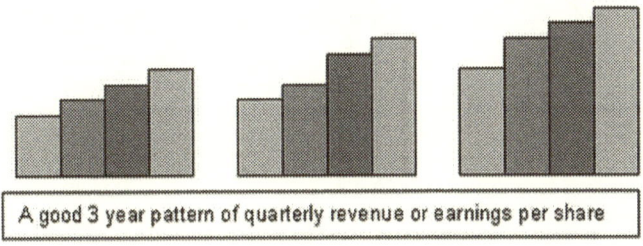

A good 3 year pattern of quarterly revenue or earnings per share

Below is another example of a company growing revenues and or earnings. The quarterly bars continue to increase year over year. This is not a stair step pattern, but exhibits the qualities of a great company.

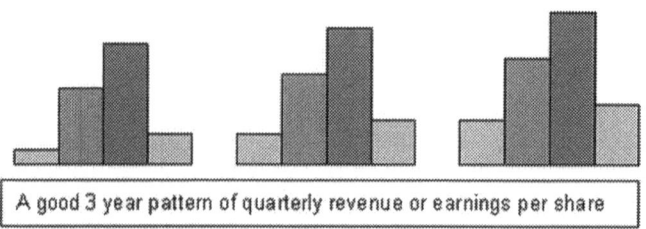

A good 3 year pattern of quarterly revenue or earnings per share

Bad and ugly revenue and EPS charts are the opposite of these. The stairs are downward, flat, chaotic, or random.

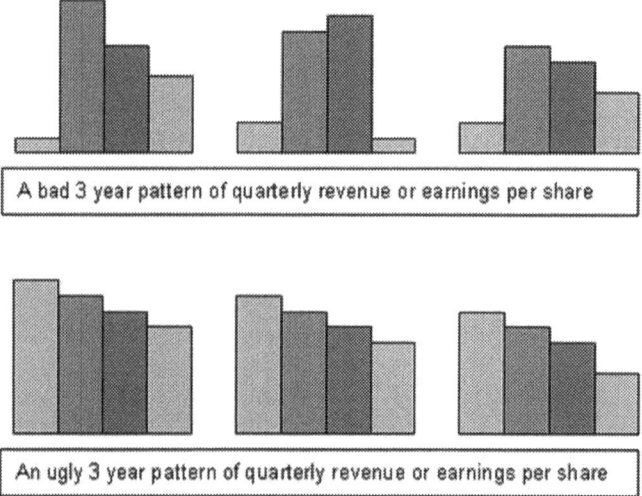

A bad 3 year pattern of quarterly revenue or earnings per share

An ugly 3 year pattern of quarterly revenue or earnings per share

6

Additional Rules

Additional Rules

There are four additional rules I use for stock selection. These add stability to my investment returns when I answer the following questions:

1. How many stocks should I own?

2. How can I determine the best industries?

3. How can I remain logical and unemotional?

4. How can I release my discretionary ideas?

How Many Stocks Should I Own?

The number of stocks held in a portfolio greatly influences both risk and return and is similar to the accelerator pedal of an automobile. How fast do you want to drive? Holding more stocks can reduce risk and return. Holding fewer stocks can increase risk, volatility, and return. If you hold the five hundred stocks of the S&P500, there is no way to beat the index—you can only tie it. Even one hundred shares will mimic the daily return of the S&P. Holding more shares does decrease volatility; this is a double-edged sword as returns are also decreased.

You may be asking yourself, "Andy, why don't I buy one or two stocks?"

You increase the mathematical risk of ruin as you approach owning a single stock. You might get lucky, pick a winner, and have excellent results. You might get unlucky, pick a loser, and have your investment snowball and evaporate into nothing. Too much or too little of a good thing can be dangerous. You need to find a balance where you're comfortable. Earlier I asked how fast you'd like to drive. This is a metaphor for your risk tolerance:

55mph—twelve to fifteen stocks
65mph—ten to twelve stocks
75mph—eight to ten stocks
85mph—six to eight stocks
95mph—four to six stocks

These are rough guidelines for the number of stocks to hold. Historically I've held eight to twelve stocks; I'm moving toward the seven or eight range which better matches my risk tolerance. You must look in the mirror and decide if you are risk tolerant or risk adverse and then choose accordingly. It's better to err on the conservative side. The fewer number of stocks held, the greater the volatility of your returns. The higher number of stocks held, the lower the volatility of your returns.

These guidelines apply best to a person already trading, or an investor with a large chunk of change now entering the market. Most people begin investing slowly, and add to their portfolio each year. In the United States and Canada, the governments encourage investment through tax deferred retirement accounts. In the U.S. we have the IRA or Investment Retirement Account, and Canada has the RRSP or Registered Retirement Savings Plan. Currently IRAs allow an annual investment limit of $3000. This amount changes from year-to-year and varies from plan to plan. Please check with your tax advisor to learn more about IRAs and RRSPs.

If you invested $3,000 this year, you would not purchase 12 stocks. The commission penalty is high and would negatively impact returns. Assuming a $20 commission per trade, here is the percent cost of commission.

12 stocks	$240 commission	8.0% cost
10 stocks	$200 commission	6.7% cost
8 stocks	$160 commission	5.3% cost
6 stocks	$120 commission	4.0% cost
4 stocks	$80 commission	2.7% cost
2 stocks	$40 commission	1.3% cost

It's difficult to earn back the eight percent commission. You would have to beat the index by eight percent in order to tie it. These fees are too high. If I were investing $3000 each year, I would purchase three stocks yearly for the next three years, for a total of nine stocks. I would then increase the size of those nine positions in the following years. Buy purchasing three stocks, this gives me a clean $1000 per stock. The commission per trade is $20 per $1000 or two percent. This is a reasonable rate.

How can I determine the best industries?

Some investors prefer purchasing shares from the leading market sector. I prefer a more stable approach to industry selection. I don't believe in one best industry, instead, I diversify. My rule is:

Never purchase two stocks in the same industry.

During the dot-com crash I got poked in the eye with a sharp stick. I was holding two semiconductor stocks and both stocks got whacked. I was holding Qlogic Corporation (NASDAQ: QLGC) and Vitesse Semiconductor Corporation (NASDAQ: VTSS). I noticed both price charts were strongly correlated. The stock prices moved up and down simultaneously. This was essentially a double bet on the semiconductor sector. When you double your bet, you double your risk. It's easier to see this effect in futures trading.

You might trade wheat. Chicago wheat trades on the CBOT, Minnesota wheat trades on the MGE, and Kansas wheat trades on the KCBOT. You could purchase one or all of these separate wheat contracts. These wheat commodities are highly correlated. Buy purchasing more than one, you're basically doubling or tripling your wheat bet.

Because of the correlation between stocks in the same industry, I try never to purchase two stocks from the same industry. As of today, I own eight stocks in the following eight industries:

Internet Software & Services
Wireless Communications
Regional—Mid-Atlantic Banks
Diversified Electronics
Medical Instruments & Supplies
Apparel Stores
Education & Training Services
REIT—Retail

I'm about to purchase two more stocks from:

Diversified Machinery
Medical Appliances & Equipment

The two medical industries are similar, but I believe the product lines are diverse enough so I am comfortable holding both stocks.

How Can I Remain Logical and Unemotional?

I want to be logical like Star Trek's Mr. Spock when I trade. Emotions are dangerous as they can lure us into acting irrationally. The rule I use to remain emotionally unattached to my holdings is:

Never buy stocks you're emotionally invested in.

If you love cars, you might want to avoid purchasing auto stocks. If you live for computers, you might want to avoid purchasing computer-manufacturing stocks. Avoid buying stocks you're emotionally invested in. If you own such stock, you might be tempted to hold onto it too long when it's going down, because you know in your heart that it's going to turn around soon. If you're about to purchase such a stock, you might be tempted to buy double the amount, because you can just "feel it in your bones" that it's going to be the next huge winner. These are not rational decisions, but emotional ones. Emotion has no place in trading. I avoid buying stocks I care about.

I like to play poker. I remember peeing my frilly white panties when poker.com (BB:PKER) began trading in 1999. Yes, I foolishly bought a stock under $10. I watched PKER go up a few days, and then I watched it go down—way down. My heart was saying, "I love poker! Everyone loves poker! This is going to be the greatest thing on the Internet ever!" I could not get out of this trade. I was emotionally invested in the stock. I think I finally sold after a 90% loss. Ouch. Never buy stocks you're emotionally invested in.

I admit I'm human and get tempted. I felt guilty buying The Mills Corporation (NYSE: MLS) earlier this year. I live near the Mills Mall in southern California, and I like seeing the parking lot full of shoppers. This stock met all of my screening criteria and I never shop at the mall. I buy everything online. I decided it was safe to own this stock.

How Can I Release My Discretionary Ideas?

Mechanical trading systems are boring. There are few decisions to be made and there is little room for creative thought. Boredom can dangerous. You might be tempted to continually change or adjust your stock picking criteria to stay entertained. To build in a creative checkvalve, I allow myself to purchase one stock for reasons other than those found using my mechanical system. This discretionary purchase is usually a promising new company that hasn't reached profitability. I place a bet on their future success. I limit this activity to one stock, this amounts to between 10% and 15% of my total portfolio value. I've held up to two stocks purchased in this manner, but consider this more risky. This rule can be stated as:

Release your discretionary ideas by picking one stock non-mechanically.

Customize by Toggling Three Switches

The stock selection rules described in the previous chapters can be adjusted to match an investor's risk tolerance. These three parameters can be increased or decreased:

1. Minimum stock price

2. Minimum percentage

3. Quantity of stocks held

Minimum Stock Price

I select $20 as my minimum stock price. I realize this is an extreme stance. You might wish to reduce this figure to $15, or $12, or $10. The lower the value, the greater the risk you take. You will produce more stocks in the screened results since this relaxes the parameter. You could also increase the minimum price upward. I believe $20 is on the high side and little or nothing will be gained by increasing further.

Minimum Percentage

On the simple three-rule 20/20/20 screen, I set the minimum values to 20%.

1. Net profit margin is greater than or equal to 20%

2. EPS growth year vs. year is greater than or equal to 20%

    On the five-rule screen, I set these minimum values to 15%.

1. Return on equity is greater than or equal to 15%

2. Net profit margin is greater than or equal to 15%

3. EPS growth year vs. year is greater than or equal to 15%

4. Revenue growth year vs. year is greater than or equal to 15%

These values can be adjusted higher or lower to best meet your needs. A higher minimum value will tighten the parameters and produce fewer results. A lower minimum value will loosen the parameters and produce more results. I prefer 15%, 20%, and 25%. Companies with 10% aren't exceptional. Companies with 25% or greater are rare. I adjust the criteria based on current market conditions. In a bear market, I'll loosen the parameters. In a bull market I'll tighten. My goal is to have the screens produce a short list of 50 to 150 companies. I adjust to meet this goal. By lowering the settings, risk levels are increased.

Quantity of Stocks Held

As stated earlier, the amount of stocks held will influence both your risk and return. Nine or 10 stocks is a good number to hold as your portfolio gets larger. You may choose to hold more or less stocks to meet your risk tolerance and investment return needs. Holding fewer stocks creates additional volatility and greater risk.

Three Rules Used by Exceptional Investors

I trade stocks a certain way. You might call this "my" style. There are thousands of successful investors and no two investor's trade exactly alike. Next, are three rules you might consider based on the ideas of three exceptional investors. I don't use these rules. It's important to understand that there is more than one way to find winning stocks. These investors are:

William J. O'Neil
David and Tom Gardner
Martin Zweig

These investors trade differently and use slightly different rules that match their styles. Here are three rules you might consider based on their techniques:

Institutional Sponsorship

William J. O'Neil, author of *How to Make Money in Stocks* writes, "It takes big demand to move supply up, and the largest source of demand for stock is by far the institutional buyer."

O'Neil picks stocks that are owned by mutual funds, pension funds, or hedge funds etc. O'Neil wants to see three to 10 mutual funds sponsoring a stock. Some stock screening tools offer the parameter "% Held By Institutions" or "% Institutional Sponsorship." If I were going to add Institutional Sponsorship to my screener, the rule would be:

Institutional sponsorship is greater than 50%

Small Caps

David and Tom Gardner, authors of *The Motley Fool Investment Guide* write, "Since 1929, small caps have, as a group, well exceeded the overall returns of larger stocks."

The Gardner's classify small capitalization growth stocks as stocks in the $50 million range to $500 million range. The market capitalization for any stocks is the total dollar value of all the outstanding shares. Market cap is calculated by multiplying the number of shares times the current stock price per share. Some stock screening tools offer the market cap parameter. If I were going to add the small cap criteria to my screener, the rules would be:

1. Market capitalization greater than $50 million

2. Market capitalization less than $500 million

P/E Ratio

Martin Zweig, author of *Martin Zweig's Winning on Wall Street* writes, "Soon I began to understand the role of earnings in valuing stocks. Also becoming clearer was the relationship between the price and earnings, the P/E ratio."

The P/E ratio can also be called the "multiple." This is the last closing price divided by the latest 12 months' earnings per share. Investors such as Zweig avoid both stocks with very high or very low P/E ratios. I don't use the P/E ratio, but many successful investors do. If I were to state two P/E rules, they would be:

1. P/E ratio is greater than 15

2. P/E ratio is less than 35

P/E is affected by market conditions, and I would adjust upward or down accordingly.

7

Sample Stocks

Eight Stocks I Currently Hold

It's December of 2003, and I'm currently holding eight stocks in my portfolio. I found them using my five-rule screen. Once I purchase a stock, I exit the trade based on price performance. I do not exit a trade if the stock fails to meet the screening criteria after the purchase. For example, if I bought XYZ Corporation and their net profit margin fell to 11%, I would not sell for failure to maintain the screen rules. I would sell based on poor stock performance.

These are the stocks I currently hold. This is not a recommendation to buy.

Company Name	Stock Symbol	Date Purchased
Apollo, Inc.	APOL	11/21/2001
Chico's FAS, Inc.	CHS	03/06/2003
The Cooper Corporation	COO	10/28/2002
International Game Tech	IGT	10/04/2002
Mobile TeleSystems OJSC	MBT	10/17/2002
The Mills Corporation	MLS	11/21/2002
Virginia Commerce Bancorp	VCBI	08/11/2003
Amazon.com, Inc.	AMZN	02/24/2003

As of December 22, 2003, these holdings have realized a return year to date of 70.9%. Please note my overall return is not this high, since it doesn't factor in the stocks that were sold this year. When these sold stocks are added in, the realized return year to date is 59.2%. This beats the three indexes, even edging out the strong NASDAQ. Past performance is not proof of future gains. A one-year track record is not statistically significant. I've been trading for the last 10 years. I was a seat-of-the-pants emotional investor until the dot-com boom gave me the whack. This rude awakening was the stimulus I needed to develop the complete, logical, and mechanical system I now use.

You may have noticed that I've held many of these stocks for a year or more. I prefer to never sell a stock; this would mean it's always headed up. I only sell when a stock performs poorly. Let your winners run infinitely. Take your losses quickly. I never sell to capture short-term gain. This makes no sense.

As an example, if your stock goes up and you decide to take the profit and sell—now what? You sold a great stock that may have kept going up. Those kinds of stocks are hard to find and now you have to find another. You found the gold, so why close the mine? The sale may create capital gains issues. A body in motion tends to stay in motion, and a stock in motion tends to stay in motion. Let your winners continue to win. The time to sell a stock is when it goes down. The trend will eventually bend downward and the order to sell will be hit. Profits or losses are then captured. The market decides when a stock should be sold.

You may have noticed that Amazon.com, Inc., is at the end of the list and separated from the other stocks. This holding was purchased with my release of discretionary ideas rule. I buy everything online and have done so since 1996. I admire www.amazon.com and was flabbergasted when the stock fell under $10. I knew Amazon.com was the Internet shopping leader with the excellent shopping cart. I always shopped there. If Amazon.com were going to fail, Internet commerce would fail. I believed passionately that online shopping would become huge and Amazon.com would reach profitability. I had to place my money where my mouth was. I purchased 1000 shares. As luck would have it, Jeff Bezos is chewing bubble gum and kicking ass and he's all out of bubble gum. This discretionary purchase has fortunately performed well.

Six Stocks I Sold This Year

These are the stocks I sold in 2003:

Company Name	Stock Symbol	Purchased	Sold
Doral Financial Corp.	DRL	02/24/2003	07/31/2003
Forest Laboratories, Inc.	FRX	09/11/2002	02/14/2003
Infosys Technologies Ltd.	INFY	11/04/2002	03/07/2003

Company Name	Stock Symbol	Purchased	Sold
Mylan Laboratories, Inc.	MYL	02/28/2003	11/11/2003
Shuffle Master, Inc.	SHFL	10/28/2002	02/06/2003
Brown & Brown, Inc.	BRO	10/11/2002	07/16/2003

Three of these stocks netted a profit, two had losses, and one was basically neutral. The price trend dictated when to sell. These sold securities represent great companies. When I sell a stock, I don't hate it or love it, it's just business. I'm not mad at the stock for going down. I'll consider buying the stock again if it passes the screening criteria. I don't fear the stock because of its short-term negative price performance. I would reevaluate and consider adding it to my portfolio in the future.

I was sold Shuffle Master, Inc., (NASDAQ: SHFL) last year,. A couple weeks later, it reversed and began climbing. I repurchased this stock a week ago. Generally, the average holding time of my sold stocks is less than the current stocks in the portfolio. This is a natural part of the system, since winners are allowed to run where poor performers are sold sooner. My longer than average holding times might surprise some traders. I'm not a day trader and I don't suggest you day trade.

Brown & Brown, Inc., was a special case. I've been testing a new rule to deal with flat performance. A flat trending stock could float inside a portfolio indefinitely, hurting overall performance—I'd hate to have three pieces of dead wood. I'm currently testing a rule that would remove the weakest stock from my holdings once every 12 months. BRO was weeded because of this test. After considering all aspects of this test, I fear it leads to excessive system tinkering. I believe this test rule would do more damage than good. I don't plan on using it in the near future.

Characteristics of These Winning Stocks

The stocks I'm currently holding have several common characteristics. These include: high return on equity, high net profit margins, high yearly EPS growth, high yearly revenue growth, and a stock price of more than $20. These winning stocks have great three-month and three-year price charts.

The stocks I'm holding do not have market capitalization in common. The market caps range from $250M to $20B. They do not share a common P/E ratio. The P/E ratios range from 20 to 70. These stocks do not have institutional ownership in common. They range from four percent to almost 100%. There are many ways to pick winning stocks, and each investor does it his or her own way. I believe my method is logical and will continue to outperform the indexes over time.

8

Review

Below is a quick review of the key points contained in the first eight chapters.

The Simple Market Model

There are two methods to research a publicly-traded company: fundamental analysis and technical analysis. Fundamental analysis includes earnings, profit margins, revenue growth, financial statements, and the future projections of a business. Technical analysis deals with stock price movement and patterns. Investors often use only one of the two models when making stock selections. Why not combine the two methods? Fundamental analysis determines if the company is strong or weak. Technical analysis determines if the stock chart is strong or weak. By combining the two methods, you can place companies into one of four categories:

Weak Companies with Weak Stock Charts
Weak Companies with Great Stock Charts
Great Companies with Weak Stock Charts
Great Companies with Great Stock Charts

I believe picking great companies with great price charts gives you the best advantage for finding market winners. This section explained how to find these stocks.

Stocks Screeners and Price Charts

The first step for finding great companies is screening. Online stock screeners make quick work of dull, fundamental analysis. What makes a great company? It's my belief that great companies produce above average profits and grow at above average rate. The screening tools quickly find companies exhibiting these qualities.

The simple 20/20/20 system is a three-rule screen, which produces a short list of great companies.

1. Stock price is greater than or equal to $20

2. Net profit margin is greater than or equal to 20%

3. EPS growth year vs. year is greater than or equal to 20%

The five-rule system is slightly more complex and also produces a short list of great companies.

1. Previous day's closing price is greater than or equal to $20

2. Net profit margin is greater than or equal to 15%

3. EPS growth year vs. year is greater than or equal to 15%

4. Revenue growth year vs. year is greater than or equal to 15%

5. Return on equity is greater than or equal to 15%

These screens produce 50 to 150 publicly-traded companies. The screen rules can be adjusted upward or downward depending on market conditions. In a bear market, I might relax these parameters. In a bull market, I might tighten these parameters. Basically, I want to obtain a short list of 50 to 100 prospective companies.

Stock price charts and EPS bar graphs are then reviewed for each company on the short list. Cream rises to the top and the great companies with great stock charts are found. When examining the three-year and three-month price charts, a graph starting at the lower left corner and finishing in the upper right corner is desirable. Flatter lines are better than wiggly lines because stability is preferred to volatility. Quarterly EPS bar graphs should be increasing from left to right. A stair step pattern headed up and to the right is good to find. Stair steps are not the only good pattern because some companies have seasonal revenue streams. The key is finding EPS increasing in each quarter from one year to the next.

There are Many Ways to Pick Winning Stocks

There are thousands of successful investors and no two investors pick stocks in the exact same manner. I'm confident with my selection techniques. If you agree with my ideas, this stock picking system may work for you. You might use the system as presented in this section or create your own variation. I encourage you to read more books on the stock market to learn the various ways different investors pick winners.

PART II
Entering and Exiting with Stops

9

Trading Range

Trading Range

The trading range is the area where a stock fluctuates between the highest and lowest transaction prices during a specific period of time. The trading range is the volatility of a stock's price. I use the trading range to determine when to buy and when to sell a stock. I also use it to determine how much stock to purchase. By incorporating the trading range into the trading system, better trades are made that are custom fit for each stock. No two stocks trade identically. Stocks rarely share the same volatility.

The technique described in the next few chapters, channel breakouts with buy and sell stops, has been described in previous investment books. I once spent an afternoon with market wizard, Ed Seykota and he taught me the basics of this method. Some of the most successful stock and futures traders use variations of this trend-following technique as a basis for their investment systems.

To find the trading range for X amount of days, find the highest price and the lowest price on a given stock chart. Here are a couple examples. This is the 90-day stock chart for Microsoft Corporation (NASDAQ: MSFT).

Chart courtesy of StockCharts.com

The highest high is right around 29.75 and the lowest low is right around 24.75. This the trading range for Microsoft's stock in that time period. Here is the same stock chart presented in a slightly different format. The above chart shows the open, high, low, and closing price. Most investing sites don't carry that much data; they track only the closing price as shown in the chart below.

Chart courtesy of StockCharts.com

In this case, I would call the high $30 or $29.75 and the low $25. It doesn't matter which type of chart you use, just be consistent. I prefer the charts with the open, high, low, and close since you get the true highest high and the true lowest low for the last 90 days. Both charts work fine—the key is consistency.

The range will be used to set our buy stops and to move our trailing sell stops. The range incorporates market conditions and volatility into each trade.

Time Frame

The trading range can only be determined once a time frame has been selected. Seven day, 20-day, and 90-day ranges are popular trading ranges with trend followers. I prefer using a longer time frame.

Benefits of a Shorter Trading Range

• More action and excitement

• Possibly slightly higher profits in testing

Benefits of a Longer Trading Range

• Simpler

• Less work

• More efficient

• Less commission

• Less prone to human error

• Easiest to do for the rest of your life

• Tax advantages of holding periods are greater than one year

In back testing, 20-day trading ranges often produce the highest profits. Computer testing is not human testing and there are practical issues to consider. A longer view of the markets is simpler and easier to maintain. Broader time frames result in larger winning trades, experience less whipsaws, and generate less commission. A bigger range gives a stock room to run. One additional benefit of a longer trading view is the lower capital gains tax rate for holding periods greater than one year. When using a 20-day range, almost all the trades will be short term. Capital gains will be taxed at the higher rate. A trader in the 38.6% tax bracket will pay 38.6% on that gain if it was realized by holding it less than one year. The capital gains rate is 20% if the asset is held for more than one year. That's a big difference. If you're in the 15% tax bracket, it gets even better with a rate of 10%. These lower tax rates make longer trading ranges with longer holding periods attractive. More trades will be over one year when using a 90-day trading range. The 90-day range makes the system simpler, less work, and generates less commission and tax. See your tax professional for advice on trading and capital gains.

Breakouts

A breakout is a rise in price above the highest point in the trading range, or a fall in price below the lowest point. I buy a stock when it breaks above the highest high for the last 90 days. Some traders refer to the upper point in the range as a resistance level and the lowest point as a support level. I prefer not to use these terms since it gives the trading range subjective attributes that I don't believe exists.

It's often psychologically difficult for investors to buy a stock that has made new highs. When a stock makes a new high, this is often a good indication it is going higher. If a stock goes from $20 to $200, it's going to be setting new highs all the way up. I don't want to buy low and sell high—I want to buy high and sell higher. I want to buy high, hold higher, and sell only when the trend ends! Buying low assumes we can time the markets. I'm not a fortune-teller. I don't know of any successful fortune-telling investors. A body in motion tends to stay in motion and a great company with a great chart—whose price breaks into new highs—tends to continue higher.

If I were buying Microsoft in the example earlier, I'd buy it when the price hits $30. This $30 represents a new high and a breakout to the upside of the trading channel.

10

Entering Trades with Buy Stops

Buy Stops

Stops or stop orders are orders that become market orders when a particular price level is hit. A buy stop is placed above the market. I use buy stops to enter trades. I use buy stops because:

- They confirm the stock is setting a new high

- They confirm the stock is breaking out of range

- The buy stop, trading range, and sell stop, are all part of a system

- They allow orders to be entered in advance

- They help maintain a mechanical trading system

- They can prevent reentering a bear market

- They can prevent the purchase of a stock that is trending down or flat

I don't want to buy a stock and hope it will go up. I want a stock to go up and then I'll buy it. The stock must prove it's trending upward by breaking out of its 90-day trading range. By purchasing stocks in this manner, you will embrace new highs rather than fear them. No bottom fishing please; purchase stocks on their way up. Winners go up and keep going up.

Buying Stock at Market

The market order is the most common way to purchase a stock. Below is an example of a market order from an online brokerage.

Stock Symbol	AMGN
Shares	100
Transaction	Buy
Order Type	Market
Price	
Duration	Day

This example represents a market order to buy 100 shares of Amgen Inc., (NASDAQ: AMGN). This is a day order from a cash account. The order will execute instantly if it's sent during regular market hours. The trade is placed and quickly executed. The investor is then informed he or she now owns 100 shares of Amgen purchased at the current market rate. This is how the majority of trades are placed each day. If this trade were sent in after hours, most brokerages would queue it for execution at the market open the (following) next morning.

Buying Stock with a Buy Stop

Here is the same order, this time using a buy stop. The differences can be found in the Order Type, Price and Duration rows.

Stock Symbol	AMGN
Shares	100
Transaction	Buy
Order Type	Stop
Price	68.00
Duration	GTC

The stop order differs from the market order in three small ways. The order type is now stop and not market. The price box is filled in at $68.00, which is roughly $1.75 above the market. The duration has been changed from a day order to GTC. This means the order will remain active until it's cancelled or executed. By placing my buy stops above the market, it may take days or weeks before the price moves up and touches the stop. If I were using day duration, I would have to place my stop orders once per day until triggered. Day orders are erased nightly when unexecuted. GTC orders are timesavers since they remain active.

Stops are not limit orders. A limit order instructs a broker to buy or sell a stock at a specified price or better. A stop order is simply a trigger—that when touched—executes a trade. A limit order is an attempt to get the price you want for a trade. If you don't get that price, then the trade does not occur. Limit orders often result in completely missing trades. You can get trapped with a stock you should have sold. You can miss buying a stock you should be holding. I don't use limit orders. Limit orders have toilet paper written all over them.

Below is the recent 90-day chart for Shuffle Master, Inc. The highest high is approximately $36.5.

Chart courtesy of StockCharts.com

If I were to purchase 100 shares of this stock, the order would be a buy stop order priced at $37 GTC.

Buy stops prevent purchasing a stock that is about to trend downward or continues trending flat. It's frustrating to purchase a stock and watch it head south. This can happen. Using a buy stop helps minimize this occurrence because a stock breaking into new highs is more likely to continue trending upward.

Buy stops prevent purchasing stocks in a downward trending or bear market. I witnessed this first hand during the false recovery stages in the years that followed the dot-com crash. In the big bear market, there were several stocks I wanted to purchase. No one knew where the bottom was. I set my buy stops and watched. There were several false recoveries and my buy stops were not hit. The market sank lower and lower. My buy stops rarely triggered and I avoided larger losses. I would have been poked in the eye with a sharp stick several times if I had purchased these stocks at market. Buy stops appear counter intuitive in a raging bull market when every stock trends upward. Don't fret. Buy stops are a defensive tool and prevent heart attacks when the screaming bear comes to town.

11

Exiting Trades with Sell Stops

Sell Stops

Once again, stop orders are orders that become a market order when a particular price level is hit. A sell stop is placed below the market. Reasons to use sell stops include:

- Limit losses

- Preserve profits

- Know when you are getting out before you get in

- Discipline

- Sleep at night

- Remove emotional decisions

Charles LeBeau and David Lucas, authors of *Technical Trader's Guide to Computer Analysis of the Futures Market* write, "The truth is that the entry is probably one of the least important ingredients in a complete and well-designed trading system. We assert that the real key to profits is knowing how to exit."

I agree with these authors. I want to know when I'm going to sell a stock even before I buy it. Stocks and futures are not identical financial vehicles, but do share many similar characteristics. Most books on the stock market deal with picking stocks. Investors need a complete approach to trading. This approach must encompass picking stocks, entering trades, exiting trades, money management, and discipline.

Using a sell stop insures I'm following my plan with discipline and logic. There are no emotional decisions to be made in the heat of battle.

Selling Stocks at Market

The most common way to sell a stock is, again, the market order. Below is a simple sell order for International Business Machines Corp., (NYSE: IBM). If you were holding this stock and wanted to sell, your market order might look like this at an online brokerage:

Order	Shares	Symbol	Price Type	Price	Term
Sell	100	IBM	Market		Day

This is an order to sell 100 shares of IBM at market, which is "good for the day." If you send this order during market hours, it will execute quickly and your stock will be sold.

Selling Stocks with a Sell Stop

Buy stops and sell stops save time and energy by releasing us from having to watch the market every minute of the day. Here is a 90-day IBM chart:

Chart courtesy of StockCharts.com

Using the three-month chart above, IBM has a highest high near 100 and a lowest low near 87. If I just purchased this stock, I would then enter my sell order.

Order	Shares	Symbol	Price Type	Price	Term
Sell	100	IBM	Stop	87.00	GTC

Like the buy stop, there are three small changes. The price type is now stop and not market. There is a price entered in the price box which was previously unfilled. As soon as the market touches this price, this trade becomes active and the shares are sold. The term is now GTC.

12

Linking the Range with Stops

Initial Risk

The sell stop can also be called a Stop Loss. It limits losses and therefore limits risk. There are two types of risk associated with any trade: initial risk and equity risk. The initial risk is the difference between the price you paid for the stock and the sell stop. In this EBay Inc., (NASDAQ: EBAY) example the trading range is between $66 and $50. I would place my buy stop at $66 and once in the trade, I would place my sell stop at $50. If I were purchasing 100 shares, the initial risk would be 100 times ($66-$50) equals $1,600.

Chart courtesy of StockCharts.com

My loss is limited to $1,600. I'm ignoring commission and slippage to keep the examples simple. Please note that commission and slippage might make the loss $30 to $60 greater in this instance. It's reassuring to know the worse case scenario before entering the trade. Knowing the initial risk will help make a better trading system.

Equity Risk

Equity risk is the difference between an open trade's market price and the price of the current sell stop. Equity risk increases as our profitable trades improve. Sell stops are used to protect both initial risk and equity risk. The initial sell stop is determined with the trading range or channel. If the trade improves, the sell stop will trail the stock upward, ratcheting in profits as it goes. This traps equity and limits the risk of the trade.

Using the EBay example, assume that EBay continues to $100. Using a 10% trailing stop, if EBay reverses and goes down 10% from its highest high, then the stock will be sold. At $100, if EBay drops to $90, this triggers a 10% trailing stop and the stock is sold. The equity risk on this winning trade is 100 shares times ($100-$90), equals $1000.

Trailing Stops

The trailing stop is a stop order set below the current stock price and adjusts as the stock price fluctuates. A trailing stop is an excellent tool for letting profits run and cutting losses short. A trailing stop is a type of ratchet, permitting motion in one direction only. If the stock price moves lower, the trailing stop does not budge. If the price drops and reaches the trailing stop, the sell stop is triggered, and the position is closed. If the stock price moves higher, the trailing stop ratchets up, continually locking in greater equity. As long as the stock price is higher than the trailing stop, the share is held.

The simplest method of determining a trailing stop is measuring with a ruler. Print out a 90-day chart for any stock and measure the distance from the highest high to the lowest low. Assume this distance is one inch. If you owned this stock and it went up in price, you would continue to measure one inch down from the highest high to determine the level at which to place the trailing stop. The ruler method works fine, but there are simpler and more accurate methods to determine a trailing stop.

13

Three Effective Trailing Stops

Trading Range High-Low Price Difference

Below is a three-month chart for Nvidia Corp., (NASDAQ: NVDA). I define the buy and sell stops as marks a little above the highest high and a little below the lowest low. You could be more accurate and select a mark one penny above the high and one penny below the low. I prefer to eyeball it.

Chart courtesy of StockCharts.com

In this case, I would choose $24.5 as my point above the highest high and $15.5 as my point below the lowest low. An effective trailing stop is the price difference between these two figures, i.e., $24.5 minus $15.5 equals $9. If I were to purchase Nvidia with a buy stop of $24, I would then trail the stock upward and move my sell stop, always $9 from the highest high as the stock proceeded upward.

New High	New Stop (high minus 9)
$25	$16
$26	$17
$30	$21
$50	$41

As a trade improves, the sell stop is moved to the new high, minus the price difference between the initial high and the low point picked for the channel. I move my stops once a week—every Saturday morning. It only takes 10 minutes. This type of trailing stop is easy to use and maintain.

There is a mathematical drawback with this method. This stop is based on the arithmetic price difference and not the percent price difference. As the trade improves, this stop continually tightens. This is not just ratcheting, but a continual reduction in the distance to the high. It's easiest to show this anomaly with an example.

Imagine you're going to buy a stock with a trading range between $3 as the high and $2 as the low. I know, I know…never buy stocks under $20. The rule can be broken this one time for the sake of learning. The difference between the highest high and the lowest low is $1. You can trail the stop upward, moving $1 under the highest high. It becomes clear that the range is not only ratcheting, but also shrinking as the stock increases in price. Eventually, the stock has to be stopped out since there is no room left to fluctuate; the range percent gets squeezed.

New High	New Stop	Range Percent (high/low minus 1)
$4	$3	33%
$5	$4	25%
$10	$9	11%
$20	$19	5.2%
$30	$29	3.4%
$50	$49	2.0%
$99	$98	1.0%

When the stock was first purchased, the low was 33% less than the high. If this stock climbs to $99, the better stop would be $66, mirroring the opening range. The stop of $98 is equivalent to a 1% range and very tight. This is an extreme example. It's rare for a stock to go from $3 to $100 in a perfectly smooth fashion, but it can occur. Be aware of this weakness for the arithmetic price range trailing stop.

Overall Percent

Another simple and effective stop is the overall percent based stop. This method cuts losses by selling stocks when they fall a certain percentage from the highs. You might choose 10% as your stop loss level.

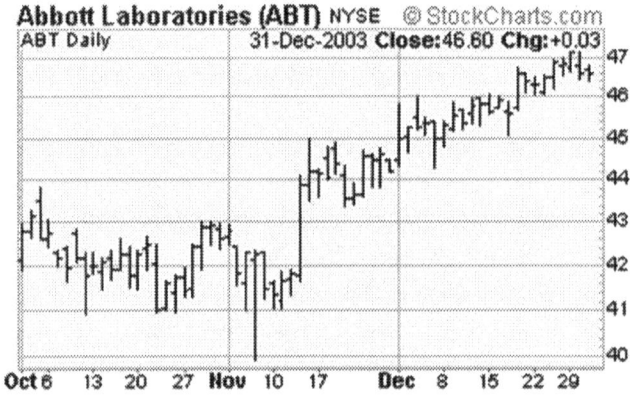

Chart courtesy of StockCharts.com

In the chart example above, I would enter this trade using a buy stop of $48. If this buy was triggered and Abbott Laboratories (NYSE: ABT) continued moving upward, I would position my stop loss 10% under the highest high.

New High	New Stop (0.9 times high)
$48	$43.2
$50	$45
$60	$54
$70	$63

The percent method is simple and effective. It's easy to calculate. It does not continually tighten like the earlier price range method. This stop has its own weakness. There is no easy way to determine the best percentage level. Stock volatility is directly affected by time, market conditions, industry category, and individual stock characteristics.

Many traders who use this method are not aware that the percent level determines how long you hold each stock. A tight percentage stop of five percent will have you buying and selling stocks more frequently than with a 15% stop loss level.

Below are closing price charts for three stocks (based on 90 days of data) at the end of 2003.

Chart courtesy of StockCharts.com

Chart courtesy of StockCharts.com

Chart courtesy of StockCharts.com

Company	High	Low	((high-low) divided by high)
Brown & Brown, Inc.	33.10	29.71	10.24%
Qlogic Corporation	58.43	47.01	19.55%
Forest Laboratories, Inc.	62.51	47.12	24.62%

The volatility of each stock is different. There's no single value that matches the range for all three stocks. Ten percent is a good choice for BRO, 20% works for QLGC, and 25% would work for FRX. Momma Bear's porridge was too cold, and Papa Bear's porridge was too hot. To use this method, I'd pick the average percent volatility for the current stocks in my portfolio. If you choose this technique, you'll end up trading more volatile stocks sooner since the stop is too tight for them. You'll trade less volatile stocks later since the stop is too loose for them.

Pro-Level Percent

This trailing stop combines the two previous methods, excluding their weaknesses. The stop is tailored to the volatility of the individual stock. This is the trailing stop I use. Instead of using a single percent, the low is divided by the high for each stock.

Company	High	Low	
Brown & Brown, Inc.	33.10	29.71	89.76%
Qlogic Corporation	58.43	47.01	80.46%
Forest Laboratories, Inc	62.51	47.12	75.38%

You can calculate this stop by hand or with a spreadsheet. I update my stops once a week. If I were holding Brown & Brown, Inc., (NYSE: BRO) and it moved up to $40, the stop would be $40 x 0.8976 = $35.90. This method of trailing stop incorporates each stock's individual volatility, making for better trades. If these stocks move higher, here is how the stops would trail.

BRO

New High	New Stop (0.8976 times high)
35	31.46
40	35.90
45	40.39

QLGC

New High	New Stop (0.8046 times high)
60	48.28
65	52.30
70	56.32

FRX

New High	New Stop (0.7538 times high)
65	49.00
70	52.77
75	56.54

14

Risk Reduction Through Allocation

The Trading Range and Risk

When using the buy stop, sell stop, and range, each trade has an exact financial risk, known before entering the transaction. This risk is directly related to the low-high percentage.

Chart courtesy of StockCharts.com

In the example above, Sharper Image Corporation (NASDAQ: SHRP), has nudged $34 on the high and $23 on the low. I would place my buy stop at $34.5 and my sell stop at $22.5, just slightly above and slightly below these points. The range is $12. If I were to purchase 100 shares of SHRP, my initial risk is $1,200. The cost of the stock is $3,450.

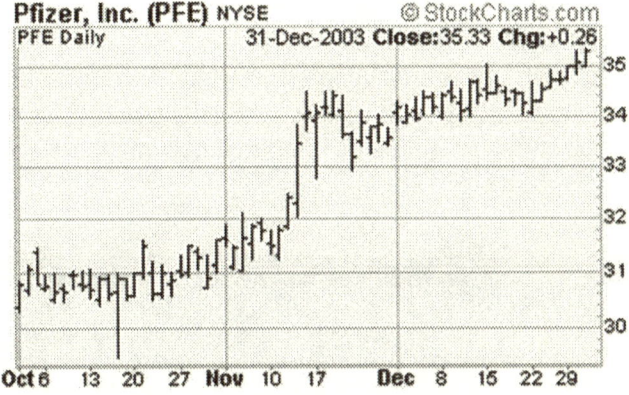

Chart courtesy of StockCharts.com

In the example above, Pfizer Inc., (NYSE: PFE) has neared $35.5 on the high and $29.5 on the low. I would place my buy stop at $36 and my sell stop at $29. The range is $7. If I were to purchase 100 shares of PFE, my initial risk is $700. The cost of the stock is $3,600.

Notice the price for both stocks is almost identical ($3,450 vs. $3,600), but the risk is different ($1,200 vs. $700). This is because PFE trades in a tighter range than SHRP. If you were trading a $35,000 portfolio consisting of 10 stocks, you could purchase $3,500 of each. The weakness of this plan is that some of the stocks will be of higher risk to the portfolio. A calculator or quick spreadsheet can help distribute the risk more evenly.

Spreadsheet Examples

stock	high	low	diff	shares	initial risk	cost
A	46.00	35.00	11.00	95	$ 1,045	$ 4,370
B	18.00	11.00	7.00	243	$ 1,701	$ 4,374
C	21.00	13.00	8.00	208	$ 1,664	$ 4,368
D	28.00	19.25	8.75	156	$ 1,365	$ 4,368
E	17.75	11.75	6.00	247	$ 1,482	$ 4,384
F	36.75	28.75	8.00	117	$ 936	$ 4,300
G	36.00	30.75	5.25	122	$ 641	$ 4,392
H	30.60	22.50	8.10	143	$ 1,158	$ 4,376
						$ 34,932

Above is an example of a portfolio containing eight stocks with a total value of $35,000. If you purchased $4,375 of each stock, the initial risk would vary from $641 to $1,701. Stock B represents more than double the initial risk of stock G.

To add stability to my portfolio, I balance initial risk when entering new trades. In the chart below the initial risk is the difference of the high, minus the low, multiplied by the shares.

stock	high	low	diff	shares	initial risk	cost
A	46.00	35.00	11.00	100	$ 1,100	$ 4,600
B	18.00	11.00	7.00	150	$ 1,050	$ 2,700
C	21.00	13.00	8.00	130	$ 1,040	$ 2,730
D	28.00	19.25	8.75	125	$ 1,094	$ 3,500
E	17.75	11.75	6.00	200	$ 1,200	$ 3,550
F	36.75	28.75	8.00	150	$ 1,200	$ 5,513
G	36.00	30.75	5.25	225	$ 1,181	$ 8,100
H	30.60	22.50	8.10	150	$ 1,215	$ 4,590
						$ 35,283

In the above spreadsheet, I guess the values in the "shares" column until the initial risks are approximately even and the portfolio total value hits my target—in this case it's $35,000. You can do this with a calculator but it's fast and easy making guesses with a spreadsheet. My good friend, David "Math Ninja" Chidley, solved the formula for determining the exact equal initial risk. His spreadsheet formula made it easy as cake.

stock	high	low	diff	Shares	initial risk	cost
A	46.00	35.00	11.00	103	$ 1,138	$ 4,757
B	18.00	11.00	7.00	163	$ 1,138	$ 2,925
C	21.00	13.00	8.00	142	$ 1,138	$ 2,986
D	28.00	19.25	8.75	130	$ 1,138	$ 3,640
E	17.75	11.75	6.00	190	$ 1,138	$ 3,366
F	36.75	28.75	8.00	142	$ 1,138	$ 5,226
G	36.00	30.75	5.25	217	$ 1,138	$ 7,801
H	30.60	22.50	8.10	140	$ 1,138	$ 4,298
						$ 35,000
					1138	$ 35,000

The formula used to calculate the $1,138 in this instance was:

= 35,000/ (46/11+18/7+21/8+28/8.75+17.75/6+36.75/8+36/5.25+30.60/8.10)
= 1,138

For math lovers, below is the e-mail David sent me.

Hey Andy,

I sorted it out for you. See the attached sheet. I have added a third table below yours. There are two constraints in your problem.

1. The sum of the costs equals $35,000

2. Risk is constant

$\text{Cost}_A = \text{shares}_A * \text{high}_A$

$\text{Risk} = \text{shares}_A * \text{diff}_A$

combining the above

$\text{Cost}_A = \text{Risk} * (\text{high}_A / \text{diff}_A)$

Now, constraint 1 says that sum of costs equals $35,000, so we can write:

$\text{Risk} * (\text{high}_A / \text{diff}_A) + \text{Risk} * (\text{high}_B / \text{diff}_B) + \ldots + \text{Risk} * (\text{high}_H / \text{diff}_H) = 35,000$

The only unknown is Risk, so we can solve the equation.

Hope that helps,
David

Real World Example and Notes

Assume you have a $9,000 portfolio with three stocks. I'll use SHRP and PFE from above and add Red Hat Inc., (NASDAQ: RHAT). Here are the values from a 90-day chart at the end of 2003.

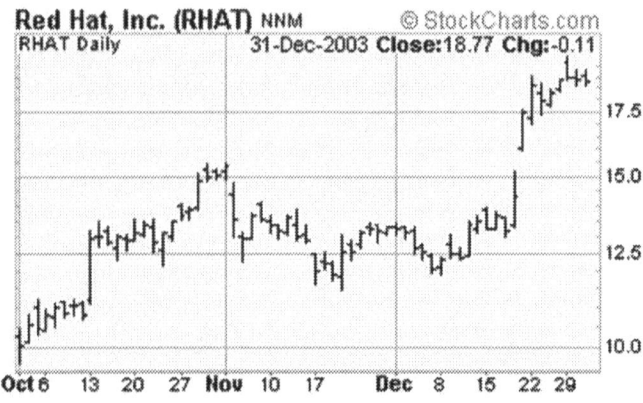

Chart courtesy of StockCharts.com

The spreadsheet below has three parts. The top section shows an even distribution of $3000 per share. The initial risk is not evenly distributed. The middle section is my share guesstimate to distribute the initial risk evenly. The third section uses David Chidley's formula to nail the exact amount of shares to perfectly distribute initial risk. Balancing the initial risk improves the stability of your portfolio.

stock	high	low	diff	shares	initial risk	cost
SHRP	34.50	22.50	12.00	87	$ 1,044	$3,002
PFE	36.00	29.00	7.00	83	$ 581	$2,988
RHAT	20.50	9.00	11.50	146	$ 1,679	$2,993
						$8,983

stock	high	low	diff	guess	initial risk	cost
SHRP	34.50	22.50	12.00	80	$ 960	$2,760
PFE	36.00	29.00	7.00	130	$ 910	$4,680
RHAT	20.50	9.00	11.50	80	$ 920	$1,640
						$9,080

stock	high	low	diff	david	initial risk	cost
SHRP	34.50	22.50	12.00	77	$ 918	$2,640
PFE	36.00	29.00	7.00	131	$ 918	$4,723
RHAT	20.50	9.00	11.50	80	$ 918	$1,637
						$9,000
					918	$9,000

Notes

This risk balancing technique is more common in futures trading because trades are made on margin and the account is almost never fully invested. Stock market accounts are often fully invested. This technique offers less benefit when adding a single stock to an existing portfolio since the value for the new investment may be fixed. This method might better be used to choose between three stock candidates, seeking the one that best matches the risk of the current portfolio holdings. Risk allocation becomes more of a factor when purchasing two or more stocks at the same time.

I do not adjust for risk once a trade is in motion. Balancing initial risk is to be done before purchasing two or more stocks. Once I'm in a trade, initial risk is no longer a factor. As a stock goes up, it naturally becomes a greater percent of the portfolio. From the example above, assume PFE and RHAT trend flat, where SHRP trends upward to $100. Your stock bundle would have $4,680 of PFE, $1,640 of RHAT, and now $8,000 of SHRP. SHRP is now a larger percent of the total portfolio. SHRP represents a greater equity risk. That's perfectly fine. You must let your winners run. I do not adjust for risk after entering the trade. I adjust for initial risk before purchasing stocks.

This year I plan to reduce my holdings from 10 stocks to eight. I'll use a variation of this technique to evenly allocate the capital generated from the sale to the remaining stocks in my portfolio.

15

Up, Down and Flat Markets

Up Markets

Bull markets are exciting! The easiest markets to trade are Up Markets. In an up market, all is right in the world. The birds are chirping and the sun is shining. Ah yes…life is good. You will be fully invested and your trades will be constantly making new highs. At the end of each week, you will review your portfolio and move your stops as necessary. In a bull market, you may wish to tighten your parameters when screening for stocks. More companies do well financially, and more stocks perform well. The danger of an up market is the intoxication of being right and thinking you can do no wrong. It's difficult to just sit.

Avoid the temptation to adjust your trading rules. Avoid placing wild bets. Anytime you're emotional, it is a bad time to fiddle with your investment plan. Bull markets are as dangerous as bear markets in this respect. Enjoy the ride. Keep your emotions in check.

> *"…irrational exuberance…"*
>
> —Alan Greenspan, Federal Reserve Chairman

Down Markets

Bear markets are painful! Down markets will test and retest your resolve. You'll constantly have doubts. Will this market ever recover? You'll have anxiety about your investment plan. You'll be tempted to believe the gloom and doom gurus. It takes discipline and conviction to ride out an extended bear market. Have a long-term view of the markets.

Historically, the markets have trended higher for the last 70 to 100 years. You must believe in the markets and believe in yourself. If you don't, you won't be able to take the pain. If you can't take the pain, then perhaps another investment alternative would better match your risk tolerance. You must believe in your trading ideas. It's next to impossible to believe in the advice of a guru when things get tough. It's difficult to have deep convictions based on the information provided in one book. Ongoing reading, studying, and thinking about your trading ideas will give you the resolution to endure nasty bear markets. You must live and die by your own sword and to do this, you must believe in your plan and understand the reasons that you follow it.

Bear markets will test your mettle. The dot-com crash had me hiding in my cave. I didn't want to leave my home or visit with friends because I just wanted to pout. The false recovery whipsaws toy with your emotions. During the last bear market I, fortunately, believed in the markets and I believed in my trading ideas. After three difficult years, finally there was light at the end of the tunnel. Yeah!

When screening for stocks during bear conditions, you may want to relax the screening parameters. Fewer companies will be doing well financially. Fewer stocks will have good charts. Many of your stocks will get stopped out. In fact, all of your stocks may get stopped out under strong down trending conditions. Stop buy orders, sit on the sidelines, and never get triggered. Finally, when they do get triggered, they reverse, sink, and get stopped out under a false recovery.

New holdings might go up for a week and then slam down as bad news shakes consumer's confidence. Sell stops make bear markets more tolerable. An investor lives with relentless anxiety if he or she chooses not to use stops. Do I stay invested? Should I get out tomorrow? Things might get better? Making decisions under duress is a difficult task Sell stops take the edge off bear markets.

Some analysts will not buy breakouts in a bear market; however, I will. No one can predict the future. A whipsaw false recovery is impossible to distinguish from a true recovery. The 90-day channel is long enough to minimize false recoveries.

Down markets test us all. Be prepared for these tests. The best preparation is discipline and conviction that comes from knowledge, research, and planning.

Flat Markets

Sideways markets are frustrating! Existing trades tread water. Stop buy orders are rarely triggered. The market lollygags up and down in a range, not wanting to continue into new territory. Uncertain consumer confidence and investor indecision pervade the financial news. Sideways markets are neither exciting nor painful—they are boring. Hang tough.

Chart courtesy of StockCharts.com

This is a 10-year chart for the Dow Jones Industrial Average. This graph has bull, bear and sideways portions. There is a strong bull trend from '95 through late '97. Late '98 through '00 was the madness of crowds and the tech bubble. The market went sideways with a downward slant from '99 through half of '01. The bear came to town from late '00 through all of '02.

My investment goals remained the same during all market conditions—beat the indexes. In an up market, I want to beat the indexes. I want to beat the NAS-DAQ, the Dow, and the S&P. This is sometimes difficult with a hot NASDAQ tech sector.

In a flat market, where the market is near zero percent return, I try and make five or 10 percent, picking wisely. It's not always easy to find stocks that stand out in flat times.

In a bear market, I want to lose less than the market. Often, investors feel they must make positive returns each year. This is not always realistic. It's difficult to get out of the way of a speeding freight train. If the market tanks 50%, you'll be hard pressed to find stocks in the black. A winning stock is a stock that outperforms the market. If the market sinks 20% and my portfolio sinks 10% that is a big win. In a bear market, a stock that loses less value than the overall market is a winning stock.

16

Review

The first section of this book dealt with picking winning stocks. The second section explained how to enter and exit trades, how to use trailing stops to limit equity risk, and how to evenly distribute initial risk.

Buy Stops, Sell Stops, and the Trading Range

You can look at any stock's price chart for a given period and determine a range for the highest and lowest transaction price. This range is sometimes called the trading range and can be used as a measure of volatility for that stock. Stock charts usually come in two forms. The most common charts show a single point for the daily closing price. More detailed charts show the open, high, low, and closing price. Either chart works for determining the trading range. Pick the format you like best and stick with it.

The given data period for a chart can be intraday, five day, ten day, one month, three months, one year, three years or more. Most investors use one week or one month. I use a three-month or 90-day chart. This time frame provides a larger bigger view of the stock price activity. Stronger overall trends are found, and less volatile whipsaws occur. A longer view results in less work, fewer trades, and produces less commission. Longer stock holding times can also prove advantageous with capital gains tax rules.

For any stock chart, there is a highest transaction point and a lowest transaction point. This is the stock's trading range. The range contains the volatility of that stock. I pick a point slightly above the highest high and slightly below the lowest low to place my buy stop and sell stop orders. The buy stop is priced just above the highest high point. The stock is then purchased once it breaks above its current trading range and heads into new high territory. The sell stop is priced slightly below the lowest low point on the chart. This stop is placed after purchasing the stock and limits the initial risk exposure from the trade.

Effective Trailing Stops

If the stock price continues to trade higher, the sell stop can be moved upward, following the stock as it makes new highs. This is referred to as a trailing stop. The stop now limits equity risk once a trade begins making money. There are four easy methods for calculating the trailing stop: the ruler method, the price difference method, the overall percent method, and the pro-level percent method. The ruler method is a non-mathematical way to position a stop. I mentioned it with the other three for interest's sake.

For the ruler method, you can print a 90-day stock chart and simply measure from the highest price point to the lowest. That measurement is the range used to trail the stock price as it makes new highs. If this measurement was one inch—as the stock moved higher—you would measure down one inch from the high to determine where to move your sell stop. If you like this old-school method, please use a logarithmic scale.

The price difference between the buy stop and the sell stop makes for a good trailing stop. If the buy stop is $50 and the sell stop is $40, then $10 is the distance used to trail the advancing stock price. If a stock you own moves to $70, the buy stop would be moved to $60, $10 below the new high. This trailing stop technique works well. The weakness of this method is the use of an arithmetic value rather than a percent value.

An example makes this deficiency clear. A stock has a $1 trading range if it's moving between $2 any $3 for a given time period. If this stock is purchased and climbs to $100, the stop would be moved to $99. The $1 range is appropriate for the $3 stock. The $1 range is inappropriate for the $100 stock. The trading range has been severely tightened with the advancing price.

An overall percent decline makes an effective stop. You can place a trailing stop at a certain percentage below the new high. Ten percent might be a good percent level. If a held stock declines 10% from its high, the trade must be exited. If you purchased a $50 stock, your initial stop would be 10% lower, or $45. As the stock moves higher, continue moving the stop to the level 10% less than the new high. If the $50 stock moves to $70, the stop would be moved to $63. The drawback with this method is that it's based on the assumption all stocks share the same volatility. Price volatility is not constant. Volatility varies from stock to stock, year-to-year, market condition to market condition.

The pro-level percent stop uses the channel high and low to find a volatility percent for each stock. Consider a stock with a price range between $50 and $40. The percent of the low to the high is 40/50 or 0.80. The trailing stop is therefore

80% of the price as it makes new highs. If this stock reaches $70, the trailing stop would be moved to $56, representing 80% of $70. This is calculated for each stock in our portfolio.

Allocating Initial Risk and Market Conditions

Each stock has an individual volatility range. You can evenly divide capital based on the number of stocks or based on the initial risk of each stock. An even allocation of capital is not an even allocation of risk. An example can better illustrate this condition.

In the last three months, Stock A has ranged from $10 to $90, Stock B has ranged from $30 to $70, and Stock C has ranged from $50 to $60. With a $9,000 portfolio, you could purchase $3000 of each stock. This is an even distribution of capital. This is not even distribution of initial risk. If all three stocks were to perform poorly, and trend downward after purchase hitting their sell stops, Stock A would erase a disproportionately higher amount of capital from your portfolio. Of the three, Stock A would lose $2,640, Stock B would lose $1,720, and Stock C would lose $500.

You can use a calculator or a spreadsheet to determine the quantity of each stock that would evenly distribute this initial risk. Special thanks to David Chidley for providing the math to solve the quantities instantly. You can also guesstimate with a spreadsheet and find the approximate quantities quickly. Initial risk allocation can be used when purchasing more than one stock at a same time. This procedure is only used before buying stocks. Equity risk is not balanced once trades are in motion.

Bull markets are fun, bear markets are not fun, and sideways markets are frustrating. Emotions must be kept in check under all market conditions. Trade your plan. Up markets stroke egos. Don't be lured into toggling the switches when things are going great. Sit on your hands. It often helps to tighten the parameters when screening for stocks in an up market. You'll most likely be fully invested during bull market conditions. It helps to loosen screening parameters in a bear market. During a downward trend, your stocks will lose value. You may get stopped out of all your trades. It may be difficult to reenter the market as buy stops are rarely hit. You might find yourself on the sidelines with a 100% cash position. The buy and sell stops will determine this. In a flat market, you'll tread water. Trades occur slowly. Existing trades will not meet new highs, nor will they stop out. Knowledge, confidence in your ideas, and self-discipline will guide you through the various market phases.

PART III

The Power of Compounding Interest

17

Realistic Returns

You Can be a Millionaire

"You can be a millionaire and never pay taxes. Yes, you can have one million dollars and never pay taxes. You say to yourself, 'Steve, how can I be a millionaire and never pay taxes?' First, get a million dollars."

—Steve Martin

That's my favorite quote from Steve Martin's album *Comedy Is Not Pretty*. You can be a millionaire trading stocks in your frilly white panties, but it's not easy. Investors can build a million dollar stock portfolio if they start early. Most investors have unrealistic expectations. You can take a historical look at the stock market and calculate an average yearly rate of return. Most investment authors place the return on the Dow Jones Industrial Average or the S&P500 between 10% and 15%. To be conservative, I use 10%. New investors often think they can quit their day jobs and live off the markets. Here is an income level chart based on a 10% rate of return combined with various sized stock portfolios.

Portfolio	Return	Yearly Income
$ 10,000	10%	$ 1,000
$ 25,000	10%	$ 2,500
$ 100,000	10%	$ 10,000
$ 250,000	10%	$ 25,000
$ 500,000	10%	$ 50,000
$ 750,000	10%	$ 75,000
$ 1,000,000	10%	$ 100,000

If you're trading $10,000, you're going to have a hard time buying food. With $100,000 invested, your yearly income level is still below the poverty line. You'll need $500,000 invested if you want to make $50,000 a year. Few people make their living trading since it requires a large portfolio to generate income. You can become a millionaire through investing. This is achieved with time and the power of compounding interest.

The Guru of Guff and the Guru of Guile

Are stock gurus telling the truth? You've seen their ads; the guru claims his system has accuracy and simplicity and makes bank! The guru claims a rate of return that makes me pee my frilly white panties. Earn 300% per year! Earn 20% per month! Eighty percent profitable trades! Ninety percent accurate signals! Wow! Can these rates of return be true?

In the short run, very high rates of return can be achieved with risky bets and luck. In the long run of five, 10, 20 years or more, investment rates of return are lower than most think. Below is a chart showing how $10,000 would grow over 25 years, based on various interest rates. I made the calculations with a helpful online compounding interest calculator also known as Compounded Annual Growth Rate (CAGR).

CAGR = ((Last Value/ First Value) raised to the (1/ Years) power) minus 1

Portfolio	Return	25 years later
$ 10,000	200%	$ 8,472,886,094,430,000
$ 10,000	150%	$ 88,817,841,970,013
$ 10,000	100%	$ 335,544,320,000
$ 10,000	75%	$ 11,911,082,073
$ 10,000	50%	$ 252,511,683

Oh my! I don't even know how to say some of those numbers. You probably want to remind me that I did not deduct for tax; I'm pretending the $10,000 was in a tax sheltered retirement investment to keep things easy. You can put $3,000 in an IRA each year—$10,000 is not that difficult to accumulate, growing tax-free. I believe the top number is eight quadrillion! I don't believe there are any quadrillionaires—the claims of 200% are simply lies. One hundred fifty percent makes for $88 trillion. That is a lot of money and I've never read about a single trillionaire in *Forbes*. More lies?

How about 100%? Bill Gates was the richest man on this planet the last time I checked. I believe Mr. Gates is closer to $50 billion, not $335 billion. Could these gurus be exaggerating? They are crooks! An average compounding rate of 75% turns $10,000 into $11 billion in 25 short years. I personally don't believe there are any traders compounding at 75% for 15 years or more.

Finally, we get down to 50% a year. This number seems so small compared to the rest, and yet it has the power to turn $10,000 into $250 million! I estimate there are less than a handful of traders reaching 50% compounded annually for 15 years. Some do exist—these are the Tiger Woods of trading. I doubt anyone can continue compounding at this rate for more than 20 or 25 years. The world banks will beat a path to your door when you can compound at 50% a year. The claims of most gurus are the claims of guff and guile.

Compounding Interest Goals or Targets

Return	Skill Level
5%	Grandma
10%	Average
15%	Very Good
20%	Excellent
30%	Amazing
50%	Ninja

The chart above shows yearly return rates and the skill level required to achieve them. Five percent is not difficult. I think most Grandmas could do it. Five percent is not a good yearly return. You can achieve this with most mutual funds and bonds. Ten percent is similar to the major market indexes. Ten percent can be achieved with an indexed mutual fund. The Vanguard 500 Index Fund has realized an annual return greater than 12% since inception. Fifteen percent is a very good yearly return. I believe Warren Buffet has stated he wants to stay at or above this target. So far he's been well above it. Mr. Buffet's company, Berkshire Hathaway, has earned approximately 25% a year for the last 30 years. He is the second richest man on earth. Let that be your guide. Twenty percent is tricky to achieve and few traders can do it in the long run. Compound at 20% a year and investors will hand you their portfolios for management.

On the back cover of Jack Schwager's book *Market Wizards,* it states "Michael Steinhardt, whose fund has averaged a 30 percent annual return over a twenty-one-year period!"

The back cover also mentions, "Ed Seykota, who realized an astounding 250,000 percent return on his accounts over sixteen years!"

Ed Seykota's 16-year return would be more than 60% compounded annually. These are two of the world's best traders. Returns of 30% to 60% are extremely rare. Indexed funds realize 10% to 15%. I would use that as a baseline and target upward from there.

18

Stock Market Advantages

The Power of Compounding Interest

The power of compounding interest is amazing. Compounding interest is the proverbial money press. Invest well, start early, and almost anyone can become a millionaire. For simplicity, I'm assuming these yearly investments are growing in a tax-free retirement account. The left column is the annual contribution. The middle column is the realized rate of return. The column on the right is the years necessary to accrue one million dollars.

Annual Addition	Return	Years
$1,000	10%	48
$2,000	10%	41
$4,000	10%	34
$5,000	10%	31
$6,000	10%	30
$1,000	15%	35
$2,000	15%	31
$4,000	15%	26
$5,000	15%	24
$6,000	15%	23

I'd like this chart to impress upon you the following ideas:

• The power of compounding interest can turn small, yearly contributions into a large snowball of wealth over time.

- Doubling your yearly investment shaves off only a few years. Quintupling your yearly investment only cuts the time in half. Time is more powerful than yearly contributions.

- A few percentage points can shave years off the total time.

The best time to start is now. Time is the fuel that feeds the compounding interest engine. It's never too late. If you're 65, invest now because you won't mind having a million in your late eighties. If you're sixteen, start investing now and you will become a very wealthy man or woman later in life. You even have the power to become a billionaire.

Invest steadily. Invest as much as you can afford each year. Steady investment is more important than size. Invest for the rest of your life. Invest as much as you can in tax-free retirement accounts each year.

A few percentage points mean everything. Two thousand dollars at 15% is close to $6000 at 10%. If you had one million dollars in the market today and could realize either 10% or 15%, which would you prefer? The difference is $50,000 the first year. It's worth it to read 10 good books on the stock market and take a pro-active approach to investing.

No Employees and No Customers

My wife and I used to own a sign shop. It was a great small business and we did well. We eventually sold the business to an employee. Friends often ask us, "Don't you miss making signs?" I reply, "I miss making signs…I don't miss the drama of customers and employees!"

There are many investment vehicles. One good investment is owning a small business. Thomas J. Stanley and William D. Danko, authors of *The Millionaire Next Door* surveyed America's millionaires. They discovered most millionaires achieved their wealth through the ownership of a small business. Most people are risk adverse.

I've encouraged friends and family to open their own business. Very few can take the leap. Being married with kids and a mortgage often prevents people from risking their life savings on the unknown future of a small business startup. These people do not have the entrepreneurial gene. Folks become frenzied at the mere thought of giving up that medical plan and company car. When you work for yourself, there are no guarantees. Aside from the public's aversion to risk, there is another aspect of small business ownership that constrains it with regards to the power of compounding interest.

For easy math, assume you own a small business that grosses $300,000 a year and nets $100,000. You invested $50,000 to start it up. The first year you make 100% return! Yeah! Now what? You can plow the money back into the business and grow it, but it's difficult to achieve sustained growth in a small business. They usually grow for two to five years then level off. Pretend you put all of the $100,000 in the bank each year, earning 0% interest. You save 100%. Each your return on investment gets worse.

start	end	return
50,000	100,000	100%
100,000	200,000	100%
200,000	300,000	50%
300,000	400,000	33%
400,000	500,000	25%
900,000	1,000,000	11%

The first year, your $50,000 investment turns into $100,000. You then have $100,000 in the bank and make $100,000. Each year the business makes $100,000 and you save it. The rate of return falls continuously into the future. You may say to yourself, "Andy, I can open more stores!"

Yes, you can open more stores. Operating one business is simpler than operating two. You'll have to open more and more stores at an exponential rate as you grow. Soon you aren't making widgets, but running a widget corporation. This is not a simple formula for compounding interest. You may say to yourself, "Andy, I can invest that money in the stock market!"

Yep…that's why this book is about stock market secrets and not small business secrets.

Real estate is an investment. Members of my family excel in real estate. Last month I looked up my home's value in 1977 and compared that to today's value. Using my favorite online compound annual growth rate calculator, I typed in the numbers and out a shot six percent yearly return. That's not a bad rate of return, but it was lower than I thought it would be. With real estate, you must remember to add in all the costs. Soon that six percent starts to look like four percent after property tax and maintenance. Don't forget six percent broker commission on the way in and six percent on the way out. You may say to yourself, "Andy, real estate is all about leverage!"

That's true, but I want to compare apples to apples. I don't buy the leverage argument, since I can leverage any investment. I can start a small business with a loan. I can trade stocks on margin. I can mortgage my house and trade stocks on the mortgage. Real estate is safer than the stock market because you are holding property and not paper. It makes sense that because real estate is safer, it offers a lower rate of return. The same practical growth problem witnessed with small businesses also occurs in real estate. It's difficult to grow your real estate empire endlessly. You'll have to buy more and more property at an increasing rate in order to compound interest at a continuous rate.

Bonds and CDs offer safer investments. Safe comes at a price. Bond and CDs realize relatively low rates of return.

Venture capital, the dot-com type, has cost me more money than any other investment. Try venture capital if you enjoy lighting money on fire. The biggest problem with venture capital is that the investments are often emotional. There is groupthink that occurs between investors and entrepreneurs. It's easy to leave your logic at the door and buy into the product or service. Investors, shareholders, and workers buy into the dream of going public. Most startups never get to market. The initial public offering day never comes. Venture capital is a very risky investment. Even if you become a successful venture capitalist, each year you'll need to find more and more great startups in order to compound at a steady rate.

Futures are high-risk investments. Futures are commodities, currencies, bonds, or stock indices, bought, or sold upon agreement of future delivery. Gold, coffee, oil, and treasury bonds are all futures. The futures market is enormous and dwarfs the stock market. Trading futures is risky and difficult. You might consider trading futures once your house is paid off, the kids are through college, and you've got a two million dollar stock portfolio. At that point, it's safe for you to trade futures. Futures trading, like stock trading, can achieve compounding rates that scale more easily than other investments. If the stock market is arithmetic, the futures market is calculus.

IRAs and RRSPs

Tax-free retirement accounts offer one of the best reasons to invest in the stock market. In America, we have IRAs, or Individual Retirement Accounts. In Canada, they have RRSPs, or Registered Retirement Savings Plan. IRAs come in several flavors, such as the traditional SEP, and ROTH. Traditional IRAs and RRSPs allow deductible contributions and allow earnings to grow tax deferred until funds are withdrawn. ROTH IRAs offer tax-deferred earnings. SEP IRAs are tied into employee contributions. There are different rules and restrictions for each investment plan. The standard IRA meets the needs of most people. Current rules allow for contributions up to $3000 each calendar year. Seek professional advice from your tax advisor to determine which plan is correct for you.

This next chart demonstrates the power of compounding interest when combined with a tax free retirement account. This chart is based on an annual investment of $3,000 compounding at 15% for 30 years with and without a capital gains tax rate of 15%.

	Ending Value	Ending Value IRA
Compounding Earnings	$ 676,619	$ 1,200,620
Simple Earnings	$ 177,862	$ 209,250
Amount Invested	$ 90,000	$ 90,000
Total Value	$ 944,481	$ 1,499,870

A simple IRA is worth half a million more in this example. Tax-free retirement plans are worth their weight in gold. Without the tax shelter, growth is approximately 15% less than 15% due to taxes. That's not exactly what's occurring, it's an easy way to think about it. This next chart gives a visualization of the IRA growth.

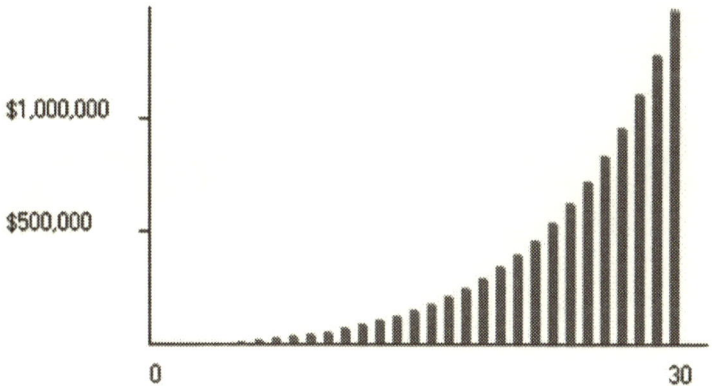

Chart courtesy of MoneyChimp.com

I'd like this chart to impress upon you the following ideas:

- Yes! The power of compounding interest really does turn small, yearly contributions into a large snowball of wealth over time.

- Tax-free growth is the same as earning a greater compounding rate of return.

- The small tax savings becomes big wealth over time.

Do the research. Talk with your tax advisor or investment planner. Tax sheltered retirement accounts often make good investment sense.

19

Easier Ways to Invest

Load and No Load Mutual Funds

You've read most of this book, and your head is spinning, your heart is pumping, and you may scream, "Andy! I don't want to play the stock market! What's the simplest way to capture the power of compounding interest while taking advantage of my IRA?"

A mutual fund is an investment company that uses its pooled capital to invest in the diversified securities of other companies. The shares are redeemable on demand at their net asset value. The fund is professionally managed. Mutual funds are diversified and portfolio diversification can provide greater safety and reduced volatility.

A Load Mutual Fund charges a fee or load when investors make purchases. This fee is used generally to compensate the salespeople selling the fund.

A No Load Mutual Fund allows shares to be purchased without a sales charge or load. I see no load funds as robbing Peter to pay Paul. The money has to come from somewhere and without a load, I suspect higher annual fees. My cynicism aside, it's generally better to start your search for mutual funds with the no loads; they seem lower cost overall.

Do your research before picking a fund. Look at the 10-year and 15-year track records of each fund. Don't be swayed by three and five-year performance graphs. Many online brokerage sites offer mutual fund screening tools. You should be able to find a good fund realizing a 10% return in the long run.

Mutual funds have historically under performed the market indices. I attribute this to their fee structures. As you add more and more stocks to the pool, the fund eventually takes on the characteristics of the market. The S&P500 is like a mutual fund of the 500 S&P stocks. The Dow Jones Industrial Average is similar and consists of 30 stocks. The funds begin to mimic the performance of the indices. The fund's disadvantage is its management fee. The fund's fee reduces the return enough that it rarely beats the indexes.

Index Funds

An Index Fund is a mutual fund that buys securities to match those tracked by an index such as the Dow Jones Industrial Average or the Standard & Poor's 500 index. The index fund attempts to achieve the same return as the general market. The funds are simpler to manage since they are run by a computer and not humans. The costs of managing the fund are minimal. An index fund will not exactly match the market's return because of the small fee, but it will come very close. An index fund is a good investment alternative for an investor who does not wish to learn about the stock market, but believes in the power of compounding interest. The Motley Fools, David and Tom Gardner, were two of the first author-investors to ballyhoo the excellent benefits of an index fund. Index funds are some of the best mutual funds available.

Diamonds, Spiders, and Qubes

DIA, SPY, and QQQ are unit investment trusts. These are traded like stocks, but act like mutual funds. The benefit of purchasing an investment trust over a mutual fund is greater liquidity and less paperwork.

DIA is the symbol of the tracking stock for DIAMONDS, a unit investment trust created to provide investment results that generally correspond to the price and yield performance of the Dow Jones Industrial Average.

SPY is the symbol of the tracking stock for spiders or SPDRs. Standard & Poor's Depositary Receipts, represent ownership in the SPDR, a unit investment created to provide investment results that generally correspond to the price and yield performance of the Standard & Poor's 500 Composite Stock Price Index.

QQQ is the symbol of the tracking stock for the NASDAQ-100 Index Tracking Stock, a unit investment trust created to provide investment results that generally correspond to the price and yield performance of the NASDAQ-100 Index.

These three investment vehicles attempt to mirror the price and yield performance of the index they represent. There is no assurance the price and yield performance of the index can be fully matched.

These tracking stocks can be traded in a regular brokerage account. The decision to purchase a tracking stock or a mutual can be financial. You can calculate the stock commission vs. fund fees and compare. Mutual funds can be more attractive to investors wanting to contribute smaller amounts to their portfolio on a monthly basis. This is impractical when buying stocks and paying commission.

Tracking stocks and index funds offer simpler stock market investment alternatives.

20

Timing, Randomness, and P/E

I Don't Believe in Timing

I believe in being fully invested; I don't believe in timing the market. The market has trended upward for the last 75 or more years; hopping in and out of the market and serves no purpose other than making brokers wealthy. I have no idea where the market is headed tomorrow or next week and I doubt anyone does. No one can predict the future, especially in the short term.

"Timing and luck are nice, but you can make more money getting in now."

—Louis Rukeyser

Louis Rukeyser tells an excellent story about two brother-in-laws named Ralph and Darth. Ralph was unlucky and always invested at market tops, but he invested early. Darth timed perfectly and hit every top. He started late, but added more capital. After 40 years, the lads' portfolios were almost identical! The moral of the story is that timing, and the amount invested, are less of a factor than overall time. Invest early and stay fully invested. Don't jump in and out of the market. You'll be wrong as often as you're right, and you will make your broker fat with commission. You'll also miss the big up moves that occur at the end of a correction.

If you pick better stocks than the overall market, then it's reasonable to assume that your returns will beat those of the index. The index has realized at least a 10% return historically. Stay invested with your winning choices and you will beat the market. If you fund your portfolio monthly or yearly, fund consistently, as soon as you have the capital. Fund now, don't wait. It's time that makes compounding interest work, not timing.

I'm not saying I'm fully invested 100% percent of the time—I'd like to be, as this would mean the market is continually moving upward. The system of buy stops and sell stops allow price action to determine when I'm in trades or on the sidelines. The buy stops get me into a trade, and the sell stops take me out. I'm fully invested 90% of the time. When the overall market begins to decline I get stopped out of one or more stocks. The new buy stops used to replace those holdings are not always triggered right away. I may end up sitting with cash until the market turns and begins trending upward again. Using channel breakouts with stops is not a magic bullet. You may miss some of the painful decline, but the price paid is missing some of the initial recovery. False recoveries can occur. Using a 90-day channel helps minimize the whipsaws. Stay invested and allow price action to determine the few times you are sitting with cash.

I Don't Believe in Random Market Theory

There exists a group of mathematicians who believe market price activity is random. The stock market is a competition; the stock market is a game. In all forms of competition, there will be players who excel at the game. Investment results are not random.

I play poker and the game I love most is Texas Hold'em. I'm not that good yet, but I'm getting better. I read, study, and practice. I give my money away in the big online tournaments. The basic rules of Hold'em are straightforward. A deck of cards is shuffled well—shuffled so well that a mathematician might even consider the cards to be randomized. Each player is dealt two cards...only two stinking cards! You might as well bet on coin flips. On the surface, Hold'em seems simple. Below the surface lies the subtle complexities, and this is the allure. Hold'em poker has little to do with the two randomly dealt cards and a lot to do with betting, psychology, and the reactions of the other nine players. I don't believe the markets are random. If statistical randomness exists, it may be one element of a more complex game.

> *"The markets are not random, because they are based on human behavior, and human behavior, especially mass behavior, is not random. It never has been, and it probably never will be."*
>
> —Jack D. Schwager, author of *Market Wizards*

I Don't Believe in P/E

P/E is the price per earnings ratio. This ratio has never been a factor in my trading. It's calculated by dividing the stock's price per share by earnings per share for a 12-month period. A stock is selling for $20 and earning $4 a share and is selling at a P/E of five.

Many investors believe stocks should be purchased below a certain P/E. I disagree. Great companies with great stock charts often have high P/E ratios. Overall, market P/E ratios change with time and market direction. If the ratio is not stable, how can it be useful? I simply see P/E as a stock popularity index. The more popular a stock, the higher this ratio becomes. I have renamed P/E to the Popularity Evidence ratio. All types of stocks are popular and unpopular. This has little predictive value when hunting for big winners.

The P/E ratio is useful with some investment techniques. I suspect if you're a value shopper, seeking great companies with weak stock charts, then the P/E ratio is a solid evaluation tool. Warren Buffet and Martin Zweig choose stocks in a certain way, often looking for these great companies at suppressed prices. Their selection criteria are such that P/E can be used to locate the bargains. I side more with William J. O'Neil and seek the riskier, but bigger winners.

"A stock's P/E ratio is not normally an important cause of the most successful stock moves."

—William J. O'Neil, author of *How to make Money in Stocks*

21

Nasty Traps

Penny Stocks

There is a nasty trap called Penny Stocks. These stocks are sometimes controlled by a den of thieves. Penny stocks are traded on the over-the-counter bulletin board (OTCBB). Penny stocks are volatile, speculative, and occasionally manipulated. Penny stocks used to refer to stocks trading for less than $1 a share—it's now more common to place the value at $5 a share or less. Companies traded on the OTCBB have minimal listing requirements, offering few safeguards for the public.

Some investors will not purchase a stock trading for less than $10. I take an extreme position and rarely purchase a stock with a value of less than $20. Penny stocks, microcap, and low-priced stocks will lure you into a nasty trap. These stocks are priced low for a reason. These companies are often struggling, are new and untested, or are manipulated.

Most IPO's debut in the $8 to $12 range. I prefer to wait until the stock has gone past the $15 mark. The big funds don't buy cheap stocks. Do a stock screen for stocks priced $10 or less and include the institutional—sponsorship parameter. Examine the results and then do the same test using stocks priced over $20. The results reveal that big funds don't want cheap stocks and neither should you. Don't buy any stock under $10. If you've got the resolve, don't buy a stock under $15. If you want to join me with overkill, don't look at stocks under $20. If a great company with a great chart goes from $8 to $100, missing the $12 from eight to twenty has little effect on overall returns. The dangers from $8 to $20 are simply too high.

Six of One, Half Dozen of the Other

It's a common desire of the public to hold a greater quantity of a cheap stock rather than a low quantity of a higher priced stock. This is a nasty trap and faulty logic. Stocks go up by percent, not by points. Johnny Q Public has $1,000 and is ready to purchase a stock for his portfolio. If offered 1000 shares of $1 stock, 200 shares of $5 stock, or 10 shares of $100 stock, Johnny usually chooses the 1000 shares of $1 stock.

Shares	Price	Total
500	$ 2.00	$ 1,000
400	$ 2.50	$ 1,000
100	$ 10.00	$ 1,000
10	$ 100.00	$ 1,000
1	$1,000.00	$ 1,000

There is no difference between the five choices. Holding more shares has no mathematical or practical benefit. One thousand dollars is $1000 is $1000. This is how Johnny Q is lured into penny stocks.

Why do stocks split? Stocks split because companies know the investing public is scared to buy higher priced stocks. Stock splits occur to appease irrational investors who believe higher priced shares are at a disadvantage.

I know some of you are nodding in disbelief. Walk to your computer and pull up a chart for Berkshire Hathaway Inc., (NYSE: BRK.A). Look at graph for 2003. Look at a 10-year graph. This is the stock for Warren Buffet's company. This stock closed yesterday at $84,800 a share. Yes, one single share is almost $100,000. Mr. Buffet is the coolest cat because he refuses to split the shares. This stock opened at the start of 2003 at $71,700 and closed at the end 2003 at $84,250. During the last 12 months, the realized return is more than 17%. The 10-year realized return is also more than 17%. This figure crushes the market indexes. Since 1990, the average yearly-realized return is even higher. Don't fall into the trap of wanting lots of cheap shares. Assuming share price is greater than $20, ignore share price when making your purchase decision.

Failing to Plan

He didn't plan to fail, he failed to plan, as the saying goes. One of my goals is to trade with a complete, organized plan. Many books on the market explain how to pick stocks. Stock picking is only a portion of investing. Even if you disagree with my ideas and logic, I strongly encourage you to think through all aspects of your trading system before investing. Does the system answer the following questions:

- Why do I want to trade stocks?

- What are the characteristics of the stocks I'm looking for?

- Why do I like this particular stock?

- How many stocks am I going to hold?

- When am I going to purchase this stock?

- When am I going to sell this stock?

The vast majority of traders can't answer the questions above. They purchase stocks on tips, hunches, and intuition. They sell stocks because they got scared watching the morning news. Being a successful investor is more than stock picking. Finding winners is one part of the complete trading philosophy.

Don't fall into the nasty trap of trading by the seat of your pants. The stock market is a serious game. You are competing against serious investors. This is risky. This is your money. You must know when you are getting out of a trade before you get in. Plan your trades, trade your plan, and you'll be on your way to having the total skill—that being a successful investor.

22

Wise Tricks

Percent vs. Points

I touched on this in the "six of one and half dozen of the other" section. Many of these issues overlap and are interrelated. A wise trick is to analyze stocks in terms of percent, not points, or dollar values. You'll often hear the financial news announce, "The Dow was up 100 points today." This information has little value. One hundred points means nothing. Sometimes the announcers will add, "The Dow closed at 10,100." Now we have two pieces of information, both of them weak. I'm not a walking calculator. I want to know the percent increase or decrease. Percent is everything; points are nothing. If the announcer said the Dow was up 1.0% today, then he or she has reported useful information. It's wise to judge investments based on percent. It's all about realized return and compounding interest.

You're at a cocktail party and you spot a gentleman in the corner surrounded by onlookers. He is a chewing a cube of cheddar cheese on a stick while sipping white Grenache. You overhear him brag how he made a tidy $20,000 profit in the market last year. Is he a good trader? His gain has shock value; the number alone is meaningless. What was the size of the cheddar chewer's portfolio at the start of the year?

Portfolio	Income	Return
$1,000,000	$20,000	2%
$100,000	$20,000	20%
$10,000	$20,000	200%

If he were trading $10,000, he realized an amazing 200% return. If he were trading $100,000, then he had a 20% year. If he were trading $1million, he gained 2%. It's the percentage of return that counts, not cash. It's difficult to analyze this trader's skills, even know his return, since one year does not make a track record and the market conditions are unknown.

This same story happened again in real life, not less than seven days after writing this. I was in my garage with a fellow car enthusiast and we talked about engines and horsepower. We also talked about small business and investments. He mentioned that his friend had done well in the markets during 2003. I asked how his friend did, and he said the lad made twenty-five large. "Oh my," I said. "How much do you think he had invested?"

After cranking the torque wrench, my friend took a breather and said, "I think he's got in the neighborhood of a quarter million invested."

Initially the $25,000 sounded like a solid gain. Once the value of the portfolio was revealed, the return was calculated at 10%. During 2003, the S&P500 was up 26.4% and the NASDAQ was up 50.0%. Percent is everything.

Logarithmic Charts

Logarithmic charts are related to percent and compounding interest. You can use a linear scale on a graph or a logarithmic percent scale. Linear graphs tell us very little. Logarithmic scaling is percent scaling where the vertical space between two points is the percentage change between those numbers.

On a log scale, the difference between one and two is the same as the distance between 50 and 100 since those both represent a 100% increase. On an linear scale, the difference between one and two is the same as the difference between 100 and 101. The former is a 100% increase and the later is a 1% increase.

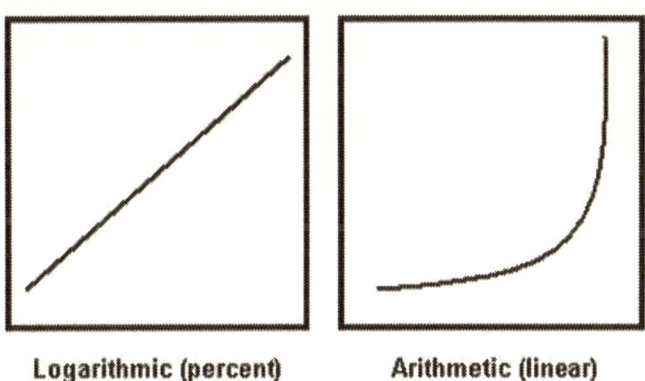

Logarithmic (percent)   **Arithmetic (linear)**

The example above is a hypothetical stock growing at 20% a year. On the log chart, the graph shows perfect, flat stable growth. On the arithmetic chart, the graph turns into a ski jump as time progresses. The line increases at an increasing rate and approaches vertical status over time. This visual representation of the stock price has less information to offer compared to the graph on the left.

It's a wise trick to always use log scale on your price charts.

The 80/20 Rule

In 1906, an Italian economist named Vilfredo Pareto discovered 20% of the people owned 80% of the wealth. The 80/20 rule means that the small 20% are critical and the larger 80% are trivial. This phenomenon is observed in science and business. This phenomenon will also occur in an investment portfolio. If you're holding 10 stocks, you may discover that two of your stocks make the big moves. Twenty percent of your portfolio will be the substantial force behind your gains. This is normal. Be aware that your stock picks will generally not grow evenly. Let your winner's run. The losers will be weeded out. It's a wise trick to understand where your big gains will come from. Twenty percent of your portfolio will make as much as 80% of your gains.

23

Learn More Secrets

Books

I treasure non-fiction books. The information in books is awesome and inexpensive. If you gain one piece of knowledge from a book, it's paid for itself multiple times. If you're going to play golf on the pro tour, I suggest you frequent the driving range. If you're going to trade equities, I suggest you read as much as you can about the stock market.

Here are three books I recommend reading. These authors are excellent investors, and know the market in their own way. Each one trades differently. For the first book I suggest William J. O'Neil's. He describes his stock selection approach he created by studying the 500 biggest stock market winners from 1953 to 1993. Starting with the greatest winners, he worked backwards, finding similar characteristics shared by big gainers. He created the legendary C-A-N S-L-I-M method. O'Neil's acronym describes the seven characteristics shared by great performing stocks before they make their biggest moves.

David and Tom Gardner, "The Motley Fools" take a practical and fun approach to investing. These lads are sharp, humorous, and provide readers with the tools needed to beat the wise men of Wall Street.

Martin Zweig is one of the most respected stock pickers and market forecasters of our time. His disciplined trend following approach succeeds.

How to Make Money in Stocks—William J. O'Neil
The Motley Fool Investment Guide—David and Tom Gardner
Martin Zweig's Winning on Wall Street—Martin Zweig

Here are three investment classics that belong on every investor's bookshelf. These books are timeless and a joy to read. The more things change, the more things stay the same. Human nature is refreshingly consistent.

Where Are The Customer's Yachts?—Fred Schwed, Jr.
Reminiscences of a Stock Operator—Edwin Lefèvre
Extraordinary Popular Delusions & the Madness of Crowds—Charles Mackay

Here are my last three favorites. Chilton's *The Wealthy Barber* is a practical guide for financial planning. Start young, max that IRA, pick a good mutual fund, and let the power of compounding interest work its magic. Schwager's *Market Wizards* is awesome. This book is hard to put down. Jack D. Schwager interviewed some of the best traders of our time. These are the world's best investors; people who compound at 25%, 30%, and even 50% a year. They all trade differently. Dr. Van Tharp's book, *Trade Your Way to Financial Freedom* is thick and chunky. This is a complete, systematic, and mathematical approach to system testing and trading. It's a great read.

The Wealthy Barber—David Chilton
Market Wizards—Jack D. Schwager
Trade Your Way to Financial Freedom—Dr. Van K. Tharp

Web sites

Here are three Web sites with great stock screening tools:

MSN Money—Stock Screener
http://moneycentral.msn.com/investor/finder/customstocks.asp

Yahoo! Finance—Stock Screener
http://screen.yahoo.com/stocks.html

Quicken.com Stock Screener
http://www.quicken.com/investments/stocks/search/full/

I really like the tools available at MSN Money. I do the majority of my research there. Here are three additional sites I use often:

StockCharts.com
http://www.stockcharts.com

BigCharts.com
http://www.bigcharts.com

Investors.com
http://www.investors.com

BigCharts.com has excellent charting tools. Investors.com is the Web site for *Investor's Business Daily* newspaper and offers many investment tools. StockCharts.com has exceptional charting tools. *Stock & Commodities* magazine recently published their 2004 Reader's Choice Awards. Reader's picked StockCharts.com as the best technical analysis Web site, with BigCharts.com as first runner-up, and Investors.com as a semi-finalist. These are great Web sites.

Newsletter, Newspaper, Brokers

The newspaper I read each morning while sipping my coffee is *Investors Business Daily*. The front page and page two are filled with important financial events from the previous day. I want my news fast, financial, and concise, and *Investors Business Daily* gives me this.

One thing that kept me optimistic during the last bear market was Louis Rukeyser's *Wall Street* newsletter. Rukeyser's overall market wisdom kept me calm. I wanted to panic. I wanted to jump ship. Rukeyser's logic and critical thinking kept me rational.

There are many good online brokers. I use Harris Direct and I'm pleased with the service. My wife and I were actually with PC Financial Network way back in the old days. PCFN then became DLJ Direct. DLJ then became CSFB Direct. CSFB was then purchased by Harris and is now Harris Direct,. E*TRADE, Ameritrade, Datek, and Charles Schwaub are also good choices. Read reviews and ask a friend or two who they use.

http://www.harrisdirect.com
http://www.etrade.com
http://www.datek.com
http://www.charlesschwab.com

24

Great Returns

Section 1—Stock Picking

Wow. It's the last chapter! Here is a quick review of the three sections followed by my final comments. In the first section, I described how I pick stocks. I use both technical and fundamental research to find stocks that should outperform the market. The stocks I want to own represent financially superior companies with great looking stock charts. I don't bargain shop; I look for the best. Online stock screening tools make searching fast and easy. I scan by using a few simple rules. I believe simplicity makes for a heartier trading system. The five rules I use are:

1. Previous day's closing price is greater than or equal to $20

2. Return on equity is greater than or equal to 15%

3. Net profit margin is greater than or equal to 15%

4. EPS growth year vs. year is greater than or equal to 15%

5. Revenue growth year vs. year is greater than or equal to 15%

I tweak the screening parameters based on market conditions. The criteria above will produce a short list of stocks. I then examine the three-year and three-month price charts for each symbol on the short list. I use a logarithmic scale on all charts. I want to find the charts starting in the lower left corner, moving to the upper right corner, while exhibiting as little volatility as possible. I take stocks that pass the chart stage, and then examine their revenue and EPS bar graphs. I look for the bars to steadily increase with time, year over year, when comparing quarters. I work through the list until I find the six to 10 equities that best meet my criteria. I prefer to purchase stocks in different industries to avoid correlation. This increases the robustness of the system.

Section 2—Entering and Exiting Trades

It's easy to get into a trade; most people can't get out. In the second section of this book, I look at the trading range for any stock during a 90-day period. This range is used to determine when the stock will be bought and when it will be sold. Just above the highest high of the range is where I place my buy stop order. Just below the lowest low of the range is where I place my sell stop order. I enter a trade when the stock makes a new high, breaking up and through its 90-day channel. Breakouts often foreshadow a continued run up.

The trading channel is used to create a trailing stop. Once a trade is in motion, I move my sell stop based on the size of the channel. Three simple trailing stop techniques are price difference, overall percent, and pro-level percent. I use the pro-level percent technique. This method divides the channel high by the channel low to get a percentage figure. This number is used to calculate the stop for each stock. If a stock has been fluctuating between $100 and $80, the sell stop would be 80% of the new high. If this stock moved to $120, the stop would be moved to 80% of $120 which is $96. This style of stop incorporates a stock's individual volatility into each trade.

The buy stop, sell stop, and trading range methods, automatically determine when an investor is in or out of the market. In an up market, the buy stops are usually triggered and an investor becomes fully invested. In a down market, the sell stops are usually triggered and the investor often holds a whole or partial cash position. Trading range can also be used as a risk allocation tool for dividing capital between new stock purchases.

Section 3—The Power of Compounding Interest

Many investors have unrealistic expectations—the sky is the limit with many market gurus. They are crooks or, at the very least, confused. Realistic returns can amass a fortune over time with the power of compounding interest. Almost anyone can become a millionaire if they start early enough and achieve an average rate of return. You could even become a billionaire. If a 16-year-old began investing $3,000 a year in an IRA that realized a 17% return, he or she would reach billionaire status at age 85. It would not be easy, but it could be done. This is the power of compounding interest.

The great thing about stocks as an investment is growth is easily managed. It's difficult to maintain high levels of return with a small business—the owner must continually find new avenues of growth. Real estate also shares this awkward growth challenge. A real estate investor must make larger and larger deals to compound at a continuous rate of return.

The American Individual Retirement Account, or IRA, and the Canadian Registered Retirement Savings Plan, or RRSP, are tax fee retirement investment accounts. These accounts offer one of the last great tax shelters. IRAs and RRSPs allow investments to grow tax-free until retirement. "Tax-free" turbo charges the power of compounding interest.

Not everyone is comfortable investing on their own. Mutual funds offer a simple alternative for those looking to utilize the benefits of an IRA with minimal effort. One of the best mutuals a person can purchase is an Indexed Fund. These funds track the overall market indices. These funds are simple to manage and charge lower fees. Historically, they outperform the vast majority of mutual funds.

Spiders, Diamonds, and Qubes are Closed-End Equity Funds. These investment trusts trade like stocks, but act like mutual funds. The decision to choose spiders, diamonds, qubes, or indexed funds, will be based on liquidity needs, investment size, market knowledge, and additional factors.

One of the biggest dangers in the stock market is Penny Stocks. Cheap stocks are cheap for a reason and must be avoided. New investors often want to hold a large quantity of a low-priced stock rather than a small quantity of a high-priced stock. There is no advantage to holding larger quantities of stock.

It's important to think about investments in terms of percentages and not points or absolute values. Stocks fluctuate in price, based on percentages. If you're holding 50 shares of a $20 stock, it's the $1,000 investment that increases or decreases. Percent growth is the reason to use logarithmic scale rather than arithmetic scale on price charts.

If you're going to buy real estate, open a small business, or trade stocks, you must have a plan. Before buying a stock, you must know when and why you're going to sell that same equity. Think through all aspects of your trading strategy before making any trades. Answer the tough questions now, not under the stress of difficult market conditions.

Read, read, read, and read some more. Books are cheap and jam packed with incredible information. The stock market is a competition. You can get good at the game and compete with the best. Knowledge will make you a better player. No two trader's trade in the exact same manner and no two books describe exactly the same stock selection methods or risk management techniques. There is more than one way to become a successful investor. Learn several ways and find the style that's right for you.

Great Returns

Great Companies, Great Charts is intended to offer investors innovative trading tools for achieving great returns.

Often times the media makes the stock market out to be frighteningly complex, and controlled by the elusive "insider." The stock market is made up of people like you and me. Stocks move up and down for fundamental and technical reasons. The market model in chapter 1 provides a simple and logical framework to divide publicly-traded companies into four groups. It's easier to achieve great returns by selecting companies that exhibit strong fundamental and technical characteristics.

Picking the best stocks is one element of a successful investing strategy. A complete system should also provide answers to these questions:

When should I buy?
When should I sell?
How much should I buy?

Trading well, is as much about self-discipline, as it is about the "system." Daily subjective decisions are often detrimental to long-term investment returns. A rule-based, trend-following system, creates an atmosphere that encourages self-discipline; this offers investors the best chance at great returns!

I continue to be fully invested in the markets. In the strong up market of 2003, the indexes had the following returns:

NASDAQ	+50.0%
S&P 500	+26.4%
DJIA	+25.3%
AMEX	+42.4%

Using the techniques explained in this book, my stock portfolio was up +61.9% in that same period. Today is February 27th, 2004, and the year-to-date returns of these indexes are:

NASDAQ	+1.32%
S&P 500	+2.97%
DJIA	+1.24%
AMEX	+6.89%

My stock portfolio is currently +7.33% ytd 2004.

Legal Disclaimer No. 2

The above statements have not been audited. No financial statements in this book have been audited. There are frequently differences between theory and actual results subsequently achieved by any particular trading system. Theoretical trading ideas do not involve financial risk, and no theoretical trading ideas can account for the financial risk in actual trading. Past performance is not an indicator of future performance. The stocks I'm currently holding, have held in the past, and will buy in the future, do not represent a recommendation to buy, hold, or sell that or any other equity. The risk of loss in trading stocks can be substantial.

I want to leave you with one last thought…in the last 60 days, I've made just two trades.

> *"After spending many years in Wall Street and after making and losing millions of dollars I want to tell you this: It never was my thinking that made the big money for me. It always was sitting."*
>
> —Edwin Lefévre, author of *Reminiscences of a Stock Operator*

Index

0-595-31275-6

www.ingramcontent.com/pod-product-compliance
Lightning Source LLC
Chambersburg PA
CBHW030812180526
45163CB00003B/1249